# Jumping Ship

# Jumping
# Ship
How to Navigate
Your Way to a More
Satisfying Job or Career

## Beverly Behan

Foreword by
Angus Reid

Published in 1999 by Stoddart Publishing Co. Limited
34 Lesmill Road, Toronto, Canada M3B 2T6
180 Varick Street, 9th Floor, New York, New York 10014

*Distributed in Canada by:*
General Distribution Services Ltd.
325 Humber College Blvd., Toronto, Ontario M9W 7C3
Tel. (416) 213-1919    Fax (416) 213-1917
Email customer.service@ccmailgw.genpub.com

*Distributed in the United States by:*
General Distribution Services Inc.
85 River Rock Drive, Suite 202, Buffalo, New York 14207
Toll-free Tel. 1-800-805-1083    Toll-free Fax 1-800-481-6207
Email gdsinc@genpub.com

03  02  01  00  99  1  2  3  4  5

**Canadian Cataloguing in Publication Data**

Behan, Beverly
Jumping ship: how to navigate your way to a more
satisfying job or career

Includes index.
ISBN 0-7737-6051-2

1. Career changes.   2. Occupational mobility.
I. Title.

HF5384.B43 1999      650.14      C98-933093-1

Cover Design: Angel Guerra
Text Design: Tannice Goddard

Printed and bound in Canada

*Stoddart Publishing gratefully acknowledges the Canada Council for the Arts and
the Ontario Arts Council for their support of its publishing program.*

*To my parents,*
*John and Trudy Behan*

# Contents

# *Foreword*

In today's new economy, dramatic changes are taking place in the structure of the North American workforce, our attitudes about work, and the management of our careers. These changes all point in the same direction: careers are less permanent, but new opportunities are more abundant than ever before. Consider the following portrait of the workforce in the late 1980s: employment anxiety (a measure of the percentage of workers who fear they will lose their jobs in the next year) was relatively low, and almost 80% of those working had full-time paid jobs (the kind of permanent jobs that are often associated with "careers").

Then came the economic and sociological revolution of the '90s. Secure and well-paid jobs in areas such as telecommunications, financial services, education, and health care were suddenly made less so, as companies and public sector organizations were forced to adjust to the new rule of the global economy: Do more, better, for less.

Perhaps the most important consequence of the transformation of the economy in the '90s has been the new value that North Americans, especially younger North Americans, place on self-reliance and personal empowerment. If the competitive pressures of the global economy make it harder for companies to provide permanent lifelong careers, if a merger or acquisition can suddenly make you redundant, then the only way to survive and prosper is to take charge of your own career: to look out for number one.

It is against this background that Jumping Ship — and the need for this book — comes into play. While articles are written almost weekly admonishing people to "take charge of their careers," few offer practical advice explaining how, exactly, one goes about doing so. While the workforce of today's new economy has spent more time than ever preparing for their careers, that education is often woefully lacking when it comes to managing careers and making necessary changes. Sadly, talented members of this gifted workforce still become trapped in unsatisfying jobs, uncertain as to how to go about making a change to something exciting, meaningful, and fun that capitalizes on their talents — *and* pays them well.

One such worker in the new economy was a young woman named Beverly Behan. After seven years of university, she embarked on her career as a lawyer only to find it disappointing. No one along the road of her years of higher education had ever taught her what to do in these circumstances. So she experimented — not just once, but through four career changes. Her varied careers involved fascinating jobs — some that no one had ever heard of until Bev developed them and "sold" the idea to someone who hired her. These jobs took her into the worlds of international airlines and corporate finance. Today she works as an executive compensation and corporate governance consultant with the firm of William M. Mercer, and consults to the Boards of Directors of some of the most prestigious companies in Canada.

Along the way, Bev developed a procedure for successfully changing careers — called "Jumping Ship" because it's designed for people who are dissatisfied with their current job situation and want to move on to something better. This process is especially useful because it was developed not by an "expert" in an ivory tower but by someone who is probably a lot like you — someone who wanted to make the best of their career situation in today's new economy . . . and found out how to.

Whether you have a B.Sc., an MBA, a Ph.D., or a degree from the School of Hard Knocks, *Jumping Ship* will give you the roadmap to finding a more satisfying job. And once you learn how to jump ship, you'll never fear the spectre of a layoff or the prospect of muddling along in an unchallenging career ever again.

Readers will do well to keep this book away from their bosses, in case they get the wrong impression. Nevertheless, I suspect that *Jumping Ship* will end up in the hands of a great many supervisors, managers, and even CEOs. Some may be thinking of changing jobs themselves and for those who aren't I suggest that this book be taken very seriously — it contains an excellent digest of what you're up against in the struggle to hold on to your best and brightest employees.

ANGUS REID
Vancouver
January, 1999

# Acknowledgements

One of the main themes of this book is that other people are often pivotal in making our dreams a reality, and that it is important to say "thank you." This is something I'd like to say to all of the people who helped make the dream of writing my first book come true.

First, to my wonderful parents, John and Trudy Behan, who have been — over the years and through all of my wild ideas — the best cheering section anyone could ever ask for. Next, to Angus Reid, a friend and inspiration, who generously offered me the key contacts I needed to get this project off the ground. To Robert Mackwood and Perry Goldsmith, my agents, and to Don Bastian, Anne Brackenbury, and all of the people at Stoddart who believed in this project and took a chance on a first-time author. To Ken Hugessen, Lisa Slipp, and all of the people at William M. Mercer, who make my current working life a pleasure, and who gave me support and encouragement when I told them that I was writing this book. To Calabogie, where much of this book was written. And to the Häagen Dazs company, whose fine products sustained me through many solitary hours at the computer.

Finally, I would like to thank all the people in my life who helped shape this book. These are people who have shared with me their career-change stories, efforts, and frustrations, who figure in mine, and who contributed to this book in ways they may not even know: Spencer Dane, Shari-Lynn Peters, Rika Compton, Christopher Roehrs, Irene Winel, Holly Cameron, Rony Zimerman, Angela Tu-Weissenberger, Bill Redrupp, John McAlpine, Al Hudec, Jill Tivadar, John Lum, Bruce Wright, Catherine McGowan, Jim Mutter, Luanne Scott-Svetelj, Ruthanne Huising, Gary Poon, Rebecca Telfer, Henry King, Barb Ingle, Ken Fredeen, Tracey McVicar, Norm King, Maria Ceravolo, Johanne Gauthier, Lisa Taylor, Cathy Thoms, Catherine Skene, Rod Kirkham, Tony Rubes, Susan and Jan Rubes, Jack Major, Milt Harradence, Cheryl Daniels, Rick Miller, Eric David, Stacey Nixon, Martin and Lenore Copeland, Dave Park, Shelley Cox, Sara Burns, Karl Gustafson, Craig Allan, North Compton, Lana Quinn, Heather Hilliard, Don Sabey, Brad Nemetz, Shelagh Flowers, Marilyn Smith, Stephen Nash, and Marty Hewitt. And to Margaret Shaw-MacKinnon, my best friend since Grade One, when we made a pact that some day we would both become writers.

# A View from the Trenches

"Everyone thinks I have this great job. I know it sounds impressive and it pays really well, but there's one big problem — I can't stand it! I hate getting up in the mornings, I look at my watch all day, and I can't wait to get out of there at night. I keep thinking there must be something better. Some days I can hardly imagine anything being much worse!"

"I got passed over for a promotion, and the new project that came in last week was given to somebody else. I've really had it! I need a job where people will appreciate my abilities and let me do the kind of work I want to do instead of this dead-end stuff. I've told them for months now that I want to do design work, but they won't let me get into that. They keep telling me that I'm the 'backbone of the department.' Well, this department may just have to learn to slither along without me!"

"The writing's on the wall. The merger's completed and they won't be needing our group much longer because they already have a whole of team of people who do what we do. I think we have about six months, maybe less, before the axe swings. The whole industry's downsizing right now. Sometimes I think maybe it's just as well — I've been bored in this job for years — but I'm not sure what else I could do. And I don't have much time to find something new."

There are dozens of books out there about job hunting, career planning, and finding a new line of work. I know because I've read a lot of them in the course of my own career transitions. Most are written by psychologists and headhunters. Some are actually written by people who are unemployed (physician — heal thyself!). Any number of them contain good ideas. But very few have the ring of authenticity that comes from someone who has successfully been through the process a number of times.

In my own career transitions, and in the course of speaking to so many others, one thing has become clear: Almost nothing is more helpful for people looking to change careers and find a job than being able to talk to someone who has actually "walked in those moccasins" — someone who can give a view from the trenches.

In this book you will find many ideas, concepts, and tactics that you may have run across elsewhere. You will also find some you have probably never seen before. The key to all of them is that they have worked. But what I hope you will find most helpful is that *Jumping Ship* is practical. It should help you see concrete progress in a very short time and lead you in a direction you want to go.

## How I "Jumped Ship"

Ten years ago, I was a young lawyer at the most prestigious law firm in the city where I lived. And I was miserably unhappy. I wanted to leave legal practice and do something — almost anything — else.

Although I had spent years at university, no one there (or anywhere else for that matter!) had ever taught me what to do if, after I got out of school, I found that I didn't like what I was doing anymore. I read every book I could get my hands on and took courses on this subject. While some had good ideas, none was particularly comprehensive. Some offered suggestions on how to write a résumé, others supplied questions to ask at an information interview, and there were reminders to brush your teeth before a key meeting in still others!

I muddled along, trying different things. I was vulnerable to the well-meaning suggestions of headhunters and friends, most of whom spent more time trying to convince me of the foolishness of leaving my "wonderful job," and some of whom came up with truly appalling ideas about possible new jobs I should consider. Finally, I wearied of lashing out in so many directions. I felt like a dog chasing after the tires of every car that came down my street!

So I decided to sit down and fashion for myself what my dream job would be. To my dismay, I found that it was something entirely new that no one had ever heard of. It used Tom Peters's concepts from *In Search of Excellence* and actually implemented them at a company to improve customer service and cut costs. I wasn't even sure what the title of this new job would be. I also realized I had very little relevant background for this work, and that if I really wanted to do it I would probably have to go back to school for an MBA.

As if that were not daunting enough, I went even further and came up with a dream employer — a large international airline headquartered in my city. This airline had been through a number of mergers and struck me as a perfect organization for the type of work that interested me. But consolidation meant the airline had implemented a hiring freeze.

At this point, most people would either drop the idea altogether or the more sophisticated of them would develop a back-up plan, given the obstacles that clearly lay between me and what I believed to be "career nirvana." But I was a greenhorn when it came to changing careers. Having finally brought some focus to this process by coming up with one idea that I thought was pretty good, I didn't know of anything else to do other than push ahead until this idea became a reality.

Fourteen months later, when I walked into my office at the international airline to start the new job no one had ever heard of, everyone was surprised. And, to be honest, probably no one was more surprised than I was!

## Happy Endings Are for Fairy Tales

Now, I wish I could tell you that from that moment on, my life became a dream and I never had to consider changing jobs again. But life isn't like that. I can honestly say that I never looked back and I never, for a moment, regretted leaving my job as a litigation lawyer to work for the airline. It is also fair to say that I loved the airline and thoroughly enjoyed much of my work there. But sometimes good things don't last forever.

A few years into my employment, the airline faced difficult financial circumstances. This led me to create yet another previously unheard-of job within the airline. I worked with a "council" of labour unions and others, who sought to save the airline from bankruptcy. We put together a transaction in which airline employees would buy shares through wage cuts totalling more than $200 million, with another major airline making a similar investment. My job never had a title and covered a gamut of responsibilities, ranging from briefing employees to take the witness stand at hearings, to coordinating employees' lobbying efforts with the government, to staging public relations events.

Because 17,000 jobs were at risk, and this kind of transaction was unprecedented, we made headline news — almost on a daily basis. Our group's strategies and reporting arrangements sometimes went straight to the company's board of directors. People asked me how I ended up getting this interesting job, and when I think back it was largely by applying jumping-ship principles — only on an internal basis within the company I was already working for.

When we finally closed the deal two years later, it was clearly time for me to leave the airline. Political factions had developed over the course of the reorganization and the writing was on the wall. From the standpoint of jumping ship, this was an important experience, because now I was being forced to find something new rather than choosing to do so on my own. And I learned even more in this round!

I embarked on my third career, and to everyone's amazement I returned to law. But where I had once been a litigation lawyer, I was now setting foot in the world of corporate finance. My involvement in the airline restructuring had brought home to me the need to get some corporate legal experience, but as almost everyone predicted, I was bored within only a few months. I had known all along, however, that this job would be a stepping stone to somewhere else. I just wasn't sure where that somewhere else would be.

## My Doctorate in Jumping Ship

Sure enough, two years later, it was time for yet another change. What began as mild boredom was now a serious distaste for this line of work. Moreover, politics had again entered the scene. Several of my closest colleagues at the firm had decided to go their own way and start their own law firm, bringing matters to a head. Those of us who had not yet declared our intentions were being called upon to do so. My options were clear: I could go with them, I could stay, or I could do something altogether different. I chose the latter.

This time, I approached career change with the sophistication of a veteran. I avoided the pitfalls I had faced years before. I began with the raw process that had served me well in the past but refined it, with added dimensions. In some ways, I felt as if I was doing my doctorate on the subject of career change. But this was no academic exercise — it was a practicum in every sense of the word: it was my own career I was dealing with.

Within a surprisingly short time, I had three job offers, all representing a complete departure from corporate law. Two of them were in a field that interested me but was virtually unheard of at that time — corporate governance consulting. The third was in a completely different line of work that drew upon the government-relations experience I had gained at the airline. They were all with prestigious organizations. They all came in at or above the salary level I was seeking. And they all capitalized on my education and work background, making the most of my interests and talents.

I realized that I had come a long way since I first tried my hand at changing careers as a disillusioned young lawyer. Most important, I realized that I had now learned a process that would stay with me for all of my working life — a process I call "jumping ship." I began to share that process with others. This has mostly been informal — meeting people who are looking to make a job or career change over coffee, lunch, or after work — but I have met well over a hundred people in this context in the past two years alone. I have also taught courses to small groups of people who are looking to make changes in their careers. The response has been positive and enthusiastic — jumping ship works, which is why I decided to write this book. It's the book I wish I'd had when I made my decisions to change careers or jobs.

# The Limits of Traditional Job-Hunting Techniques

Newspaper, and now Internet, advertisements are probably the first places most prospective career changers and job hunters look. The next step usually involves headhunters. While I would never discourage anyone from using either, I would also encourage you to use these methods with an understanding of their limitations. What most people find is that the job they really want is seldom found in the careers section. Nor is it usually the first thing the headhunter suggests, although it is tempting to jump at these possibilities.

When you are unhappy in your career and the very act of dragging yourself from the parking lot to your desk is becoming a burden, just about any sort of change looks good. The glowing job description lovingly crafted by a headhunter, jumping out from the pages of your local paper or the dim light of a Web site, has definite appeal. But I suggest that, like Odysseus and his crew, you tie yourself to the mast of your ship and ignore these siren songs for just a little while. They may well land you on the rocks.

## The Classifieds

There are three distinct problems with ads that appear in newspapers and on the Internet:

1. *Too many people read and reply to them.*
   Any ad that interests you is probably being noticed by hundreds, even thousands, of other career changers and job hunters just like you. For every one of these postings there are guaranteed to be a slew of competitors chasing the job. And you can be sure that the more exciting the position sounds —

the loftier the title, the better the salary expectations, and the more prestigious the employer — the more the competition will increase. Ads for professional or senior management positions in major papers have been known to generate more than three hundred responses regularly.

You may say, "Well, I'm not afraid of a little competition." Good for you! But wouldn't it be easier to leave all that competition behind and make your job hunt into a "competition of one" for almost every position you go after? If you think so, read on, because you should learn how to jump ship.

2. *Ads discriminate against career changers.*
How many ads have you read lately that describe the experience for job positions in terms like these: "The successful candidate will have little, if any, direct experience in this field but must have a burning desire to enter this line of work and a good track record in another field of endeavour"? Does "three to five years' experience in progressively responsible positions" sound a little more familiar?

For anyone looking to make a career change, this new job is going to be their first foray into the field. Still, many people sit down at their word processors with hope and optimism, and pound out résumés in response to ads in new fields that interest them. Their impressive track records should be sufficient to attract the interest of the advertiser, who will at least grant them an interview, right? After all, a proven record of success in one field can translate into success in another, can't it?

Of course it can! But an impressive track record in an unrelated area is likely to lose out every time to direct experience. At some point, the process of weeding out the applicants who will not be granted interviews will begin. An applicant without direct experience has a far greater chance of being weeded in this kind of contest. While there are exceptions to this rule, they are generally just that — exceptions. And prospective career changers — many of whom might actually have been better candidates than those with direct experience — too often wind up with nothing more than a "Thanks for Coming Out" letter.

What you need is an opportunity to sit down with prospective employers and convince them that you have vision and passion for this new field. You need to illustrate that your experience, while not in the same field, has provided relevant skills that would be a tremendous asset. Your skills may, in fact, be more relevant than those of candidates who have simply been "working their way up." Most important, you need this opportunity to occur without the background noise of hundreds of other candidates, many with direct experience, distracting the prospective employer. In short, you need to learn how to jump ship.

3. *Ads try to convince us to consider jobs we wouldn't normally have any interest in.*

When you are unhappy in your present job or career or are actively looking for a new one, you are particularly vulnerable to the power of suggestion. Nearly everything looks better than the mundane or frustrating job you sit down to every morning. In this state, you are clearly on the hunt for something better in a hurry! So, while you may never have seriously considered becoming a public relations director for a chemical manufacturer, the ad makes it sound awfully enticing!

Do you have any burning interest in public relations or chemicals? Probably not! But many of us will try to convince ourselves that we could become interested in these areas because they seem more interesting than the brain-numbing jobs we currently find ourselves in. If you don't watch out, you may end up on this new path. And six months or two years later you'll be wandering aimlessly in to work at the chemical company wondering whatever possessed you to strike out in this direction!

Wouldn't it be better to spend some time focussing on the areas that really have potential to interest you, areas that use your background, education, and experience to best advantage, rather than jumping at suggestions on the Internet or in the newspaper? If you think so, then jumping-ship techniques may be far more valuable to you than ads.

## Headhunters Are Not Career Counsellors

Headhunters also have their limitations. They are paid to find people for jobs, not to find jobs for people. It is not the head-hunter's responsibility to place you in your dream career. Their task is to find someone with the skills and experience to fit a job opening they have been retained to fill. If you happen to walk in one day with those very skills, you can be sure they will play up the positive aspects of the job they are trying to fill in the rosiest of colours. The fact that you may be trying to escape from that field is quite another issue. They have a job to fill; you have the credentials. While most are professional enough not to counsel an obvious mismatch, finding you something better or different from what they have to offer is not their role, which is something many people (myself included for a while) don't understand. So you can easily become frustrated with or disappointed in your headhunter.

The best way to utilize ads and headhunters is to recognize their limitations and view them as elements in an overall career-change strategy — but not the *only* elements. Once you have outlined your direction and begun your research, as described in the following chapters, you can have a more focussed, and probably more helpful, discussion with a headhunter — one in which you are in greater control. You can also be much more discriminating in responding to ads. Better still, you may discover that your time is more effectively spent pursuing the jumping-ship route to career changing and job hunting.

## What's Involved in Jumping Ship?

The jumping-ship process involves a different way of looking at your career. It often means shifting priorities to make sure the horse is before the cart. I begin, then, by dispelling some of the myths and addressing some of the concerns that may be holding you back from getting on with your search. To achieve this, I outline some of the common mistakes people make in trying to change jobs or careers so that you can avoid them, and I show you how to develop your own job targets over the course of two weekends so you can get focussed and start moving ahead. Note that the goal here will be to develop job *targets* in the plural — not just one great be-all-and-end-all job goal that may leave you in the lurch. By taking the time to outline your own goals and set realistic targets, you ensure greater control over your career search.

Next, you'll learn about some simple tools of the trade that will help you organize the information you will collect so you can access it easily along the way. I will discuss how this, along with some research, can fast-track your career transition and help you contact the people who can make your career shift a reality. You'll also learn how to improve the odds of getting them to talk to you.

Finally, I provide a step-by-step guide to convincing prospective employers that they should hire you. You'll learn that your best chance of making your job target materialize at a company that "isn't hiring" — and may never have even heard of the kind of job you want — occurs when you demonstrate your value rather than ask for a job outright. I'll also suggest ways in which you can pick yourself up and keep on with the search even when you hit some of the frustrating obstacles and dead-ends that everyone encounters along the way.

## Who Should Learn to Jump Ship?

Jumping ship is a process primarily designed for those who want to change careers and embark on a new line of work. But the principles work equally well for those who want to change jobs within the same career path, and for those who are unemployed and seeking a new job which may or may not involve a career change. Whether it's a personal decision or the pink slip has been delivered, everyone can benefit from these techniques.

While not actually designed for those entering the workforce for the first time, many of the principles outlined in this book can be modified for use by recent graduates looking to start their careers on a solid footing. They can be used by people who are making an internal job shift (who wish to move into another job or line of work with their present employer), and, to a lesser extent, by those looking to start a new business or work on their own.

Because my own background is in the area of law and finance, many of the examples that I use come from these worlds and from my own personal experiences. The principles outlined, however, apply to nearly all lines of work. The concepts and tactics found in this book have been successfully used by a variety of people in very different areas:

— a secretary who developed a cartoon series and now works in cartoon production,
— a flight attendant who became a politician,
— a pilot who became a real estate developer,

— an accountant who became a restauranteur,
— a software designer who now develops career-counselling programs for high school students,
— a budget analyst who became an interior designer,
— a publishing executive who went into consumer goods marketing,
— a teacher who became a journalist,
— an office manager who became a headhunter.

You can also apply these principles to extracurricular pursuits: When I decided I wanted to write this book, for example, I used jumping-ship methods to find an agent and sell the book to a well-known publisher. I used them again to secure an appointment to the policy committee of the board of trustees of the largest museum in Canada. I also use these methods to develop new business and clients for my corporate governance and executive compensation consulting practice.

Once you learn how to jump ship, you will have developed a skill that should serve you well throughout your working career as well as in other areas of your life. But it is not a skill that you can develop simply by reading about it. You can only learn how to jump ship by doing it.

## *Why You Owe It to Yourself and Everyone Else to Find Happiness in Your Career*

Is there a perfect job out there? One where every day is filled with a burst of energy and fulfillment, completely lacking in any of the problems associated with your present job and workplace? Probably not. Is there a job out there that is going to give you considerably more satisfaction than the one you currently have? If you are reading this book, my hunch is that the answer is probably "Yes." You obviously have some serious concerns with the job you now have, and you deserve better.

In fact, you deserve the best job situation you can possibly find, and not just for your own happiness. When you find the job that best suits you, you will maximize your talents and make the most valuable contribution you can — not just to your employer but, at the risk of sounding grandiose, to the world we live in. You will also be a lot more fun around your family and friends.

Your success will inspire others — be it your friends, former coworkers, or your children. Your experience will demonstrate that it is possible to move out of a dissatisfying job or career into something more fulfilling. And the techniques you learned to make the change will be something you can share with them if, and when, they decide to change careers or jobs themselves. Nothing is more helpful to someone in the throes of a career change than the advice of another person who has "been there, done that" and been glad of it. Your example may serve to encourage many others to find greater happiness in their working lives. Finding happiness in your career is something you owe to yourself — and to everyone else.

# Getting a "Round Tewitt"

Procrastination Kills. If it came in a package, it would carry a surgeon general's warning. Of course, it doesn't kill people, but it kills time and it kills momentum, and if you don't watch out it can kill great ideas and cherished dreams. I know, because I'm a big procrastinator — a "heavy user," so to speak, of a variety of procrastination devices.

During one of my career-changing periods, a friend presented me with a circular object that he told me was called a round tewitt. "What's this for?" I asked him. And he told me, "It's to help you with your job search." "Well, how's it supposed to help?" I questioned. "I'm not sure, exactly," he replied, "but you keep telling me about this great new job that you're going to start working towards just as soon as you get a round tewitt. So I thought I'd give you one."

Most people don't procrastinate because they're lazy. When it comes to looking for a new career or job, many hold off the search for a number of reasons that have nothing whatsoever to do with laziness. Some think that their efforts will be wasted because, sooner or later, something great is just going to come along anyway — as they have seen happen for other people. Others wonder whether changing careers or jobs is really the right thing to do; they are concerned that this may be an irrevocable decision that they may not be prepared to make. And for most, looking for a new job or career comes at a time when they're already feeling disappointed and not at their best — they want to put it off until they are feeling more positive and confident.

Whatever the concern — and most people actually experience all three in varying degrees — the net result is the same: procrastination that not only defers the search, but actually contributes to a sense of vulnerability and depression. Here, then, are some practices to avoid as you embark on the process of career change.

## *The Job Fairy*

Lesser known than either Santa Claus or the Easter Bunny is the Job Fairy. You know it as that magical creature who will come along and save you from the trouble of going through the job-hunting process by laying at your door the perfect new job just when you need it most! You may never have heard of the Job Fairy, but she has many believers. They often procrastinate and put off getting started on their job hunts while they await her arrival, only to be disappointed when she fails to show up!

Frustrating, isn't it, to see the Job Fairy alight on the shoulders of others? Once, when I was looking to make a change, a friend recommended that I take a holiday. She described how she had done just that when she, too, had been fed up with her job. And suddenly, one afternoon, as she vacationed in her hotel room in Maui, she received a phone call from the Job Fairy. The Fairy was in the guise of a former colleague who had tracked her down to offer her a position as vice-president of a new high-tech company he was starting up.

How I bristled with envy as she recounted this tale! Why, oh why, I wondered, wouldn't the Job Fairy come and land on my shoulder? Why was I being forced to first go through the mental gymnastics of figuring out what I wanted to do, and then subject myself to the angst-ridden process of searching for a new career? Why couldn't the Job Fairy simply whisper in my ear as it had in my friend's, and start me along the rose-strewn path to career bliss?

Only later, when I had gone through the more difficult process of finding my own new career using many of the methods outlined in the following chapters, did I realize that I might have been the lucky one. For when the Job Fairy alights, her whisper seems so full of promise that we never stop to consider our options. We are so relieved to have a wonderful new opportunity open up amid career malaise that it hardly makes sense to do anything but jump quickly to seize this golden moment and thank our lucky stars for its arrival.

The downside, however, is that there are actually many career and job opportunities open to every individual at any given time. The Job Fairy promises only one of them. If we have not yet uncovered the others, we believe that the opportunity presented is the only one available to us. And so we jump — and feel fortunate to do so — without stepping back for a moment to consider whether that opportunity is the *best* choice.

I believe that those who endure the process of deciding what it is they really want to do, and who explore their options, are actually more fortunate than those to whom a new opportunity seems to appear almost effortlessly, because for the latter the search ends before it has even begun. If a better opportunity did exist, they would never know about it. As hard as it is to avoid envying those on whom destiny has smiled, the tougher road is frequently the one that leads to greater career satisfaction in the long run.

## *The Myth That You Can't Go Home Again*

Barbara P. has spent several years building skills and establishing herself as a marketing manager for a large company that sells coffee. She's good at her job, but lately she's been getting bored. Secretly, she yearns to make a radical shift into merchant banking, but she's afraid. Her friends tell her she should stay put, and that she'll be up for a promotion some time soon. She knows that moving off her current career path could cost her not only a promotion, but her entire career. She fears that, in spite of her experience, she'll never get another job in marketing if she fails at banking. How realistic do you think Barbara's fears really are? Will all of her marketing experience really go out the window if she ventures into banking — and then decides to return to marketing? Hardly!

One of the most daunting things about changing careers, or changing jobs within the same career path, is the prospect of finding a new job or career that is every bit as unsatisfying as the one you currently have. All the angst associated with finding the new job, starting over, and proving yourself again in a new environment would seem to be for naught. The idea is enough to make you think twice about even typing up your résumé!

This grim scenario gets even worse if you believe that you can't go home again — even if the new alternative proves unsatisfying. In most cases, your worries are unfounded, but they can paralyze you with fear and curtail your progress towards finding a more satisfying career or job. The skills and experience you have built in your current job will almost always be there for you to fall back on, even if you end up using them in a different way or with a different employer.

Ironically, I have heard many people unhappy in their work speak wistfully about a new career direction they would pursue if they lost their current jobs. It's strange that people feel they need to go through something as unpleasant as losing their jobs before they will explore more exciting career options. What often holds us back from making a move into something we are more interested in is the fear of giving up what we already have. Being fired seems to give us the freedom and courage to look at options we would not consider otherwise — because at that point, there's no trade-off and nothing to lose.

This tendency is often more acute amongst people who have a professional designation. They have spent years in university, followed by professional exams, to obtain their designation as lawyer, chartered accountant, actuary, or engineer. Not far down the career path, however, they sometimes find themselves disillusioned and unfulfilled. They yearn to try something else that would bring greater challenges and more satisfaction, but are reluctant to give up something that has consumed so much of their time and energy. Moreover, the prestige associated with these careers is often difficult to say goodbye to — professional designations often define who we are.

I wrestled with this extensively the first time I quit being a lawyer. In spite of the derision hurled at that profession, calling myself a lawyer was a source of pride. And yet I longed to be fired from my prestigious law firm. From the ashes of my crumbled legal career would rise the phoenix of an exciting new airline career! And I wouldn't have "given up," so to speak — I would have "rebuilt."

In the end, some are freed from making this decision by the arrival of the longed-for "pink slip." Even with healthy severance packages, however, it's frequently less of a positive experience than may be imagined. Others, and I would venture to say most, make the decision to leave on their own, despite the security they are giving up. While there is no sense being cavalier about throwing away a good situation for a dream, there is also no sense in being chained to an unhappy situation and forfeiting a dream just because the existing situation has not dissolved on its own. Knowing that you can go home again — at least much more easily than you may have imagined — may help overcome this hesitation. Let the skills and experience you have built to date be your security blanket — not your straitjacket.

## *The Timing Is Always Bad*

Seldom does the urge to change careers dawn upon us when we are happy and fulfilled in our lives, bursting with energy and creativity. Inevitably, it happens when we are at a low point.

That point may be the result of feeling dissatisfied with our work, unappreciated by those we work for, or tired of unpleasant office politics. Or it may be a response to what is often referred to as "the writing on the wall." Others are being promoted and given the plum projects while we continue to plod on the treadmill. The boss seems distant and increasingly critical. While no one has said anything directly, deep inside is the feeling that we may be part of an inevitable reorganization. We fight the temptation to simply leave because we have no better place to go!

In any of these situations, we find ourselves at a similar point psychologically. If the company is "downsizing" we feel rejected, unworthy, and embarrassed. If we plod along unhappily we feel frustrated and lacking in respect. In none of these situations are we at our best. Our energy level is flagging. We are disappointed, even a little bitter. And under *these* conditions, we are supposed to set about the task of selling ourselves confidently to a new employer!

Procrastination often sets in. We aren't "feeling up to it right now." We need more time, we need to feel better about ourselves. The career-change/job-search process is so laden with fears of rejection that it is terribly tempting to try to put it off when we are in such a dismal state. The most effective way out of this state, however, is to start to see some doors opening to a brighter future.

## Energy Boosters

Think of the burst of energy you will experience, however, when the job you want is yours! Imagine telling your friends and family about it! How about your coworkers or boss? One of my favourite pastimes during a career change was to begin each morning writing, and then ripping up, my resignation letter over breakfast. This little trick imbued me with the burning desire to finally deliver one of those letters! And it gave me energy to carve out some time during the day to advance my career-change/job-hunting process. Consider some of the following energy boosters and procrastination busters as you prepare to make the change.

### Accomplish Something Small but Significant in Another Area of Your Life

There are creative ways to give yourself more energy for the significant task of changing careers. One of the most effective is to accomplish something small in another part of your life to boost self-confidence. Examples include making a speech, becoming involved in a volunteer project, and learning a new sport or skill. The key is to find something that requires taking a bit of a risk and that will likely give you a "rush" to accomplish. Completing this small endeavour will provide tangible evidence that you can take risks, succeed, *and* feel good about it.

The other key is to target something that can be accomplished in a relatively short time frame. Winning an Oscar or climbing Mount Everest is not the kind of extracurricular ambition that is required here. Standing up at a meeting of city council to express a view you feel strongly about on a proposed bylaw will do. Other examples may include learning to water-ski for the first time, doing ten minutes of stand-up comedy or karaoke at amateur night, having your "Letter to the Editor" published in the local newspaper, or taking a group of preschoolers for a tour of the local aquarium.

## Give Yourself Some Small Rewards for Efforts in the Job Hunt

Throughout the career-change/job-search process, remember to take good care of yourself. When you work hard researching in the library or calling some contacts, give yourself a small reward to acknowledge your efforts — an ice cream cone, a new CD, or a long, hot bath. Big companies give bonuses and stock options as "incentive compensation" — you should provide your own "bonus system."

Make sure that these small bonuses are within your budgetary constraints, however. When Mark W. lost his job, he used his severance package to buy a new sports car. While this had the desired effect of lifting Mark's spirits, it also increased his anxiety about finding a new job as quickly as possible, and made him feel pressured to accept the first decent offer that came his way rather than holding out for something he'd enjoy much more.

## Invite People to Your "New Job" Celebration

One of the more unusual ideas for curbing procrastination is the "new job celebration." Here's how it works: Target a date sometime within the next twelve months by which you hope to have found your new career or job. Call up a handful of your closest friends (other than current coworkers and your present boss — unless you are feeling *really* confident about the target date) and invite them to your new job celebration. Have them note the date and make sure you put it prominently on your own calendar. Mailing out invitations may serve to further solidify the process and add to its reality. The impending date will often provide enough incentive to light a fire under the most complacent would-be career changer or job hunter!

But what if the new job has not materialized by the time of the celebration? You may want to have the party anyway! Update friends on the state of your job hunt. Ask them for assistance with networking, if appropriate, and set another date for the "real" celebration. This one you'll be sure to keep, if for no other reason than avoiding the embarrassment of having to reschedule it yet again.

## The "First Day on the New Job" Outfit and Other "Signing Bonuses"

Another anti-procrastination technique, generally more successful with women than men, involves buying interview clothes or a first-day-at-the-new-job outfit. Many guides will advise you to dress "as if you have the job." To get you up and working towards finding that job, one helpful tactic might be to purchase an outfit that someone in the kind of position you are seeking would probably wear. The key is this: The new outfit is not to be worn to your current job. It is to be used *only* for meeting key contacts who can hire you for the position you want, or saved for your first day on the new job. The pricier the outfit, or the more you like it, the less you will want to have it languishing in your closet. To put it to use, of course, you have to create the opportunity.

A variation on this theme — equally successful with *both* men and women — is to promise yourself a "signing bonus" in the form of a sizeable gift that you will give yourself when you get the new job. Whether it is season's tickets to your local professional baseball team, a weekend in New York, or a new set of golf clubs, it should be something you have wanted for a while and that has a significant price tag. Feel free to shop around for this item in your leisure hours (few as they may be) during the job-search process. You may want to keep a few reminders of the prospective "signing bonus" in your desk drawer or taped to the refrigerator so they can serve as reinforcement. As with the new outfit strategy, the "signing bonus" cannot be purchased until the new job is yours.

# Setting Job Targets:
# *What* Not *to Do*

With your energy levels increasing and the procrastination demons at bay, you still have some hurdles to overcome before jumping ship. Career changers and job seekers are generally pretty clear about some things. They are dissatisfied, bored, or unchallenged by their current lines of work, and most can even elaborate — often in impassioned tones and for lengthy periods — as to why. But if you ask them what type of work they would like to get into, the most common response is a blank stare and a hazy "I don't know exactly."

This, however, is a pivotal question. And it must be answered before any real progress can be made towards making a successful change. For without some idea of the eventual destination, it is impossible to chart a course. Would-be job seekers chase after every possible new opportunity, not realizing that by doing so they are putting the cart before the horse.

This is not to suggest that you need an unwavering destination from the outset. Becoming too specific too quickly is an equally dangerous practice. Still, taking the time to set a direction at the outset is a necessary prelude to an effective career search. After all, if you don't know where you're going, any road will take you there.

Questions about career direction can be difficult to answer. Some people feel they don't even know how to begin figuring out what they want to do. It's something rarely taught in schools or universities. Others are reluctant to address the question for fear of coming up with a wrong answer. Some people draw a blank — nothing at all seems to come to mind. Others, by contrast, feel overwhelmed by their options. With so many interests, they fear they won't make the right choice, and will later regret those that they forego.

People approach the question of "What is it that you'd like to get into?" as one of the great mysteries of life — akin to finding the meaning of life itself. Consequently, they undergo a tremendous amount of pressure trying to come up with the *right* answer. What most people fail to realize is that there is no right or wrong answer. Approaching the question with real thought will put most people leagues ahead of those who never bother! The only wrong answer is to avoid grappling with the question. There are, however, some approaches that should be avoided as you begin.

## The Laundry List

Frank G. lost his job when his company merged with another and operations were reorganized. Frank greeted his pink slip with a mix of fear and elation. He was worried about meeting mortgage payments, but he also knew he wanted to try a different career. Frank didn't want to make a decision before he had considered all his options. He picked up articles on hot new careers and visited headhunters and counsellors. They generated lists of potential careers, some of which promised excellent remuneration. Frank tried to work up some enthusiasm for the suggestions on the lists, but most of them left him cold. Looking carefully at the lists, he realized that these jobs might work well with his skills and background, but none had tapped into either his interests or his passions.

Many people begin the process of setting job targets by asking someone else to develop a laundry list of career options for them. While there is some merit to this approach, it has significant flaws. It reduces the job seeker's role to the relatively simple task of putting a check mark against a few items of interest in a series of alternatives generated by others. Job seekers are often convinced that someone else is more knowledgeable in the area than they are. But these lists tend to be generated on the basis of fairly superficial information — general education history and past work experience — while ignoring the less tangible but often more important questions, which relate to passion.

Be assured that *no one* is more knowledgeable about your career than you are. While obtaining some input on alternative choices from "experts" may be helpful, it's nothing more than that: input that can be added to the mix, or discarded, depending on how you respond. I know few people who are more unhappy than those who choose a career direction for which they have an excellent background, but an absolutely lukewarm level of interest.

Try to avoid selecting a new direction simply because you have heard that there is going to be tremendous potential in that field. This is one of the major pitfalls in using published articles on "hot career choices" and asking opinions from job "experts." Counsellors and writers have a well-meaning tendency to direct people to areas where they feel there will be considerable opportunity in the future. If the expanding field happens to be one that you find fascinating, it's great news. If it holds little personal interest for you, it is probably the wrong choice. You may find a job in the short term, but you are unlikely to maintain a sufficient level of career satisfaction to keep you happily engaged over the long term. Sooner or later, you may be looking to jump yet again.

Another drawback of the laundry list approach is its focus on traditional job roles. Jobs or careers previously unheard of will never make it onto that list. While the creation of an entirely new job may sound exotic, stop for a moment to consider how many job titles people have today that were completely unheard of twenty years ago. How many Web masters did you know in 1985?

The laundry list has the process backwards. It begins with established jobs and suggests that you position yourself in the one that's the best "fit." Instead, create a profile of the job target *you* would most enjoy and then determine whether a similar position exists. If it doesn't, consider who would hire you to do this sort of job and how you would convince them that it would add value.

## The Job Horoscope

A variation on the laundry list is the job horoscope — a process for generating career alternatives through vocational and personality testing. These tests can be extremely valuable in providing insights about your personality and working style, which may lead to alternatives not previously considered. But knowing that you are an ISTJ on a Myers-Briggs test and therefore deciding to pursue a career in structural engineering just because ISTJs tend to do well in this field, can turn a helpful tool into a prescription — sometimes a prescription for disaster. There are no divining rods that will provide immediate answers. Placing too much reliance on these types of career tests can be limiting. Your personal judgement is always the most important factor.

# All the Eggs in One Basket

Kelly S. was in the reception area, palms sweating, as she awaited the vice-president of the company she would soon be joining. Kelly had taken control of her career, outlined her dream job, and was now making it happen. But when the office door opened, she was ushered in and greeted gruffly by a man who, within moments, struck her as the twin brother of Darth Vader. In her wildest dreams, Kelly couldn't imagine working for such a person! Without any alternatives, however, she began to rationalize the situation in her head. Maybe he wasn't such a bad guy when you got to know him. Maybe she could get an office as far down the hall from him as possible. Or, maybe, if she travelled enough, she could avoid him.

Sam J. had a different experience altogether. He hit it off beautifully with his new boss, and after an hour of exciting conversation Sam felt as if he had just landed his dream job. Then he learned that the salary was half of what he had anticipated — and half of what he was currently earning! Sam had no back-up plan, so he was working out the compromises before he had even started. Maybe he could refinance the mortgage. After all, being happy in his work would more than compensate for the low pay. Besides, maybe it was just a starting salary. Bonuses, stock options, and a raise would surely be his in a year!

Some people know *exactly* what they want to do and they find a job target that seems both promising and fulfilling. They have clearly done some good thinking about their career direction. They are no longer susceptible to the suggestions of career ads, headhunters, and well-meaning friends and they are on their way. The only downside is that they have taken the time and effort to develop only *one* job target, and that makes them vulnerable because they have put all their eggs in one basket.

What if there is a personality conflict with the dream employer, or the salary level isn't close to expectations? What if the job is currently being done by someone else who seems unlikely to leave any time soon? What if the industry is experiencing a temporary downturn and hiring freezes abound? What if, in essence, the job target just cannot be turned into reality? Then what?

Obviously, the discouraged job seeker will have to develop secondary targets and ride into the fray once more. So why not develop those targets right at the outset instead of waiting for disaster to strike? The downside is that you may have to expend energy on an exercise that may prove unnecessary. The upside, however, is a plan that you can fall back on at any point in the job hunt should your first choice begin to lose its lustre.

We are not one-dimensional people for whom there is only *one* perfect job. We are creatures of diverse interests and knowledge bases with varied educational, work, and life experiences. These all lend themselves to the development of a range of career choices. Contrary to popular beliefs, there tend to be *more* choices the older we get. This is because we acquire more work experience and exposure to different areas of interest over time. To suggest there is only one job for us is to sell ourselves short. There may be one that strikes us as a better fit than others, but surely there are others that could become serious alternatives if the compromises required to land our dream job become extreme.

## *The Holy Grail*

After years of slogging it out in middle management at an insurance company, Gloria S. took a buyout (the company had restructured her department). She vowed she would now find the perfect job — one that capitalized on her skills and talents, and provided greater satisfaction. Gloria wanted to prove that she could do something important in the world. What she didn't want was to feel trapped and worthless in another dead-end job. A year later, having exhausted her savings and the patience of most of her family and friends, Gloria still hadn't located that dream job.

Why do people sabotage themselves in this way, devoting weeks, months, and even years to the mission of finding that elusive "perfect job" while ending up immobilized and unable to make any further progress with the search itself? Some truly fear making a wrong choice. And yet, the only wrong choice they make is to continue spinning their wheels on the question of a career direction. Sometimes, it's just a matter of taking a deep breath, making a choice, and getting on with it.

For other people, the issues are much deeper. Often their self-esteem has taken a battering over something that has happened in their working lives. They have been downsized, passed over for a promotion, or significantly underutilized in their jobs. For them, finding a new job means proving a point.

To prove this point, they must come up with a job that has considerably more prestige, money, or glamour in order to again lift their heads high. But the pressure they put upon themselves to find this glamorous job can be overwhelming and can lead them to inaction while they search for this elusive Holy Grail.

There are two dangers facing people who find themselves in this position: either they avoid the fulfilling job target for the more glamorous one that will impress friends and former co-workers, or they give up on both targets because neither offers everything they want. The first choice offers "glitter" without fulfillment, the second continues the quest for the perfect job. In the meantime, the search continues, while people around them grow weary.

Peter T., a former chief financial officer of a small public company, faced this problem after his company was acquired by a large competitor. Embarking on a new career in teaching had real appeal for Peter. A move into investment banking, however, offered much more prestige. As neither choice offered both glamour and fulfillment, he continued to search for something that could combine both goals.

At some point, the quest for the Holy Grail must end and choices have to be made — choices that will involve trade-offs. Those trade-offs are as different as the people who make them. My own tendency is to place somewhat more weight on choices that tap into your true passions and interests, and less weight on those that just look impressive. All that glitters is not gold. There is a danger that the new job may be hollow once the initial glamour has worn off. I also believe that you have a better chance of turning a job you love into a glamorous, exciting, and even prestigious venture by harnessing your passion and vision. At the same time, discounting the glitter factor entirely is often a big mistake. You need to feel good about what you do for a living. There may be ways to add some glitter to a less glamorous choice in order to come closer to having the best of both worlds.

# Job Targets 101: A Short, Self-Taught Course That May Change Your Life

I've talked a lot about what *not* to do in developing job targets, which prompts the obvious question: How do you go about developing job targets in the right way?

There is no perfect formula. Outlined below, however, is a process that has worked many times for many people. It involves a concentrated effort over a condensed period of time and should help you prevent the obstacles outlined in Chapter Three. At the same time, it should bring into focus most of the major issues that need to be addressed as job targets are developed. Feel free to modify this process to better suit your needs. I have only a few caveats:

— Establish from the outset a definite time frame for defining your job targets and schedule concentrated periods of "work time" for this process within that time frame.

— Ensure that you consider *all three* questions posed under the Job Targets 101 Curriculum in the course of your deliberations. Don't hesitate, however, to add others and to undertake whatever exercises may assist you in considering these questions to your satisfaction. Those outlined here are only suggestions. You may find it helpful to consult other books and reference materials on a number of these questions.

## The Time Frame

How long should it take to develop job targets before you begin the search process? My rule of thumb is that it should take two weekends. Some will scoff at this, noting that they have already spent weeks and months considering this question and seem no further ahead. But I'm not talking about time spent running the question through your mind. I mean two *solid* weekends spent *alone* on no other activities than contemplation of your career. In my experience, anyone who sets aside two weekends to work on developing job targets should be far enough along at the end of that time to begin the search.

What if you don't have the luxury of finding two solid weekends to devote to this purpose? There are family commitments, relationships, and extracurricular activities to consider, not to mention the worry over what your children or spouse will do while you are locked away on this project. There is no magic in a schedule of two weekends, although it works neatly, and the week-long break between them gives you time for further contemplation of important questions in a more casual manner. If this plan isn't possible, try to carve out a schedule of something like three solid hours a night for a full week, with a week off between, and another week of three solid hours a night. Or find an alternative schedule that involves roughly the same length of time with several solid hours at a stretch, and some "down time" in the middle.

The key here is to view the time set aside for this process as analogous to taking a course. Resist the temptation of trying to schedule in some thinking on this topic while doing other activities. For example, "My wife and I are going to the beach next Saturday. I'll think about this while I'm lying on the beach." Or "I enjoy going for a morning walk by the ocean. I'll be sure to spend time thinking during my walks." This is what I call casual contemplation time. It is useful and often enlightening. By all means do it. But these quiet moments waiting for a "gestalt" experience are generally not enough — and often take too long — to allow you to arrive at some decisions and begin moving forward with the job search. View these as useful but supplemental efforts.

Setting job targets takes time and concentrated effort to be effective. You need to be alone. You need the time to write and read. Mostly, you need some solid blocks of uninterrupted time to think. You would not dream of trying to learn a second language, master a new computer program, or discover how to write a murder mystery in your spare time on the beach. Call this "Job Targets 101" — a short but extremely intense course that may just change your life — and schedule time for it accordingly. It may be the most valuable course you have ever taken!

## *The Curriculum*

Setting job targets is a bit like cooking, though there is no recipe for arriving at a "right" answer. Instead, there are a number of ingredients that need to be stirred together to develop some answers that will allow you to begin the search. There are three dimensions that should be considered at the outset:

— Identify job targets (lines of work, industries that hold **passion** and great interest for you.)

— Identify areas of your work experience and education background that have provided you with some **transferable skills** that might be applicable to those job targets.
— Identify how much **money** you would like to make.

## *Money Does Matter*

Some of you may be surprised by that third bullet. If so, you'll be even more surprised when I advise you to *begin* the process with identifying the amount of money you are interested in making. This may sound incredibly mercenary. I can almost hear the howls of protest: "I want to find work I'll love! The money doesn't matter!" Finding work that you love is extremely important. But anyone who says "The money doesn't matter" is kidding themselves just a little bit. Ultimately, we should all aspire to a career that brings us *both* tremendous job satisfaction and the financial means to support the lifestyle we desire.

A study conducted by Frederick Herzberg at Case Western Reserve University in the 1960s concluded that money does *not* provide career satisfaction. It is passion for your work, feeling you are making a difference, and enjoying your coworkers and work environment that are the key components. But the same study concluded that money was one of the biggest factors in career *dissatisfaction*. If you are in a mundane, unfulfilling job where you feel like a cog in a wheel, making a healthy income will not suddenly make this brain-dead job satisfying — and no amount of money ever will. But by the same token, if you are in a job where you really feel you are making a difference, using your favourite skill set, and working in an area that is tremendously interesting, you may still become dissatisfied if it doesn't pay enough.

There are two ways to gauge whether the money is "enough." You can consider your lifestyle in absolute terms by asking how much money would be required to support your desired lifestyle. This doesn't mean asking how much you could get by on, nor does it mean outlining your wildest bank account fantasies. It requires that you think about what things are important to you in your lifestyle and what amount of income is needed to ensure you have them.

You can also look at the question by asking how much money you honestly feel you are worth relative to others and relative to the education and work skills you would bring to a prospective employer. Then consider what range of income would be required for you to feel that you are well paid in this context.

Popular myth suggests that love of work is inversely proportionate to income. We often hear of people "stepping off the career track," meaning they have taken a large cutback in pay to explore a new field. This is sometimes the case, but it is not a law of nature. There are many, many people on this planet who enjoy tremendous career satisfaction *and* very healthy incomes. Why shouldn't you be one of these?

Moreover, do not assume your initial income will be your permanent income. Sometimes, when you change careers, it is necessary to begin by taking a stepping-stone job. It pays little but affords you the opportunity to acquire skills and build experience in a new field. When you are considering the amount of money you want to make, do so in the context of what you would like to make on a permanent basis — not in terms of what the stepping-stone job is likely to offer. And consider setting some target dates for how long you will stay in that job and when you would like to be making the target income level you desire.

There is a simple reason why I believe it is worthwhile to begin developing job targets with the rather crass subject of money. Experience has shown that once this question is answered, sharper focus can be brought to other considerations. Too often, people devote considerable effort to analyzing areas where they have true passion but from which they are completely unable to make a desirable living. Let's face it, if you really feel you need a six-figure salary to feel good and have the things in life you crave, any thoughts about devoting your life to trekking in the Himalayas are likely to vanish pretty abruptly. Unless, of course, you are able to come up with some creative way to make that field yield you the money you're seeking, like running tours that use trekking as a team-building exercise for Fortune 500 senior executives.

The key to the whole question is simply this: Determine how much money you want to make. Then try to figure out how you can harness your passions and your abilities to fashion a career that would meet this financial target. Never mind that no one may have heard of the particular career path you start to bring into focus to accomplish this goal. If you believe it could yield you the money you are after, bring you into a field of work you would love, and draw upon your talents and experience, you have a winner!

### Harnessing Your Passions

Sometimes when we experience severe career dissatisfaction, we lose touch with the things that give us passion in our work. Yet all of us have experienced passion for our work at some point in our lives. Think back. When was the last time you stayed up late to finish work on something just because it was fun? Maybe it was only a few months ago or maybe it was back in school. Whenever it was, try to remember how it felt, because that was a feeling of passion for your work.

When was the last time you spoke enthusiastically with some-one about a project you were working on, an idea that you had, or a subject you were studying? Your eyes shone with intensity! You shared something that you really enjoyed. That was a feeling of passion for your work.

When was the last time you felt a tremendous sense of accomplishment for something you had achieved — whether it was a satisfied client, a finished report, or an "A" in a difficult subject at school? If there was something tangible associated with it, such as a letter of appreciation or a photograph of people involved in the project, you may have enjoyed quietly looking at it by yourself afterwards. This, too, was a feeling of passion for your work.

You have experienced it! You know how good it feels. And you deserve to feel this sort of passion as an ongoing element of your work life. So now it's time to identify job targets which harness your passions. Here are three questions that should start you on your way:

— What articles or journals do you *really* enjoy reading?
— What subjects do you get really enthusiastic about when you talk about them?
— If you could only make *one* contribution to a field of endeavour in your life, what field would you choose? Why?

When you consider the answers to these questions, try to go deep enough to identify the root of what it is that creates that sense of passion. If you have identified a real interest in history museums, don't leave it at that, ask yourself why. You may answer that you enjoy exhibits where you feel the past comes to life for visitors. What that second answer reveals is that the root of the passion stems from an interest in both people and history. In addition to museum work, you may be interested in teaching history or preparing documentaries, books, or CD-ROMs that vividly evoke that history for viewers or readers. Or maybe you have identified a passion for politics. When you ask why, you may realize that you enjoy debating socially relevant issues. If you go deeper to discover whether it is the debating or the social issues that you especially enjoy, you may encounter very different career directions.

At this point, tools like the Myers-Briggs test, and other exercises aimed at providing insight into your personality and interests, can be used effectively. As I mentioned earlier, these should not be used to arrive at specific conclusions, but as a means of helping you formulate your job targets. For example, if your Myers-Briggs profile suggests you have a high need for affiliation, it could reaffirm your preference for job targets that involve working in a team.

Harnessing your passions is the headiest aspect of setting job targets. It is a vital component worth considerable effort because you gain important insights that can assist you in setting job targets that resonate. However, it is equally important not to get lost in the "layers" of analysis that can characterize this process.

This exercise isn't about uncovering one "right answer." Even if you came up with what seemed to be the "right answer" — a job that would fully engage your interests — you would still need to determine whether you have, or can readily gain, skills and abilities in this area, and whether it can guarantee you a sufficient income level to avoid long-term dissatisfaction.

## Taking Stock of Your Abilities and Experience

Too frequently we feel doomed to having to start over in a new area by taking an entry level position. Sometimes this is inevitable. Many more times this prospect can be avoided by having a good, hard look at aspects of your background that may lend themselves to your areas of interest.

Brian N. has an interest in management consulting but he lacks the typical credentials. In his job with a software company, however, he works with many consultants. He understands consulting from a client's perspective — a valuable experience that those who follow the traditional route of MBA school to entry level job at a consulting firm, and so on up the ladder, simply do not have. Brian is also more intimately aware of the issues clients face when implementing consulting advice, and he believes he could build client rapport better than someone who has never worked on that side of the equation.

Brian has plenty to sell to a prospective employer in the consulting business even though he has never worked in that industry. There is no need for him to resign himself to an entry level job. All Brian needs is an opportunity to convince a prospective employer that his background brings a unique perspective that would add value while he learns the specifics of the job and the industry.

The key is identifying the experience and transferable skills that can catapult you into a good starting position in a new field where you may lack direct experience. Consider what elements of your background make you even more valuable than someone who came up through the usual "training grounds." What might give you a valuable perspective that most people generally lack? What specialty could you bring to bear in the new field while you learn the "nuts and bolts"? You hit pay dirt when you find experience and skills in your background that lend themselves to your area of interest, but bring something both different and useful — something lacking in the people who traditionally work in that area.

Similar transitions can be made by people who want to turn a hobby into a career choice. For example, Angela T. is a senior economist for a major bank. She studies market trends and conducts economic forecasting. She spends considerable time giving speeches on the future of the North American economy and how this could affect the investment climate. Her passion, however, is art history. She has taken numerous evening courses on art and has visited most of the world's major art museums during her vacations. She has no formal training and no degree in art history. Does Angela really need to start over, perhaps returning to university for an art history degree or cutting her current salary in half for an entry level position in a museum, in order to make a change into this field?

Think for sixty seconds how Angela's background might already put her ahead of people who traditionally enter the field. Think for another thirty seconds of the jobs within this new field that might be appropriate for her background. That same type of thinking is what you need to apply to your own circumstances.

The really good news in all of this is that we rarely develop strong passions and interests for an area unless we have had some sort of exposure to it. That exposure fuels the passion. It can also give a sense of where your skills and background can add value.

It's also true that womb-to-tomb employment is quickly becoming ancient history. The days of finishing with the gold watch at the same place where you began your first job are long gone. The 1995 *Report on the American Workforce* published by the U.S. Department of Labor cited research that showed that most people have an average of eight to ten jobs throughout their working lives. We have become a nation of "career entrepreneurs" who sell our skills and our talents in many different forums throughout our lives. As this trend has developed, employers have also come to realize the benefits of bringing someone in "from the outside" with a fresh perspective and new skills that the traditional "silo" of career development within the organization will not provide. Cross-hires are no longer rare birds.

## The Stepping-Stone Job

Sometimes there are components of your background that lend themselves nicely to the new field but there is also an obvious skill gap that will preclude you from making the entire transition in one fell swoop. In fact, when you are completely honest with yourself, you admit that this skill gap will need to be addressed before you can expect to make a serious run at the new field. If this is your situation, it may be necessary to consider a stepping-stone job.

A stepping-stone job may or may not be an entry level position. The focus is the experience this job will provide to allow you to fill the skill gap and move on. A secondary consideration, which generally comes into play if you are choosing between two stepping-stone jobs likely to yield equivalent experience, is to select the one that offers better contacts within the industry of your choice.

Never choose a stepping-stone job for the money. It may well be so far below your eventual target that the pay difference between two stepping-stone jobs becomes inconsequential. Experience is what matters. The target income level you identified in answering the first question in this process should be that associated with the final career target — not the stepping-stone job designed to get you there.

Always remember that the stepping-stone job is exactly that — a temporary but necessary stop-over on the way to your final career target. Ideally, it should *only* be taken with a definite plan in mind: how long you will stay before moving on, and what experience you need to gain. Sometimes you will need to take the initiative to ensure you are learning what you need to. If there are three things you want to learn in the job but your work seems geared to only one, make it clear at the outset that you will, at the very least, want some exposure to the other two. Be on the lookout for opportunities in those other areas and remind your employer that you are interested.

Taking a stepping-stone job often raises an ethical issue. After all, you are asking an employer to provide you with training when you have every intention of taking that training and heading off elsewhere. Does that mean you should tell the employer at the outset that you view this position as only temporary on your way to bigger and better things? My answer is "Absolutely not!"

First of all, most stepping-stone jobs are taken for a year or two, and most don't pay very well. In that year or two, I am anticipating that you are going to work hard for your employer as you learn the skills you need to acquire, providing them with pretty good value for their money in the process. Second, employers are big boys and girls. They know that intelligent, capable people in a fast-paced economy have many opportunities. Even those who begin the stepping-stone job with the intention of staying on forever can have a change of heart or find that exciting new opportunities have presented themselves.

If the organization really believes you are an asset, they may create the kind of position you are ultimately seeking. Discussions of this nature should generally only happen a year or more into the stepping-stone job. At that point, both you and the employer will have gotten to know each other. You will know if you want to stay on, and they will know whether they are willing to create the kind of job that will keep you with the organization.

Jennifer K., who had always been an avid shopper, thought it might be fun to get into purchasing. It struck her as far more interesting work than her job managing an insurance office, so she took a fairly significant drop in pay and accepted a position that would teach her the basics of becoming a buyer for a retail furniture store. For two years, she worked long hours for modest wages, keeping in mind that her goal during this period was simply to learn all she could about this new field. She began talking with a hotel chain about doing their purchasing, in a role that would involve supervising three other buyers. But before discussions got too far along, she approached her current employer and told them she felt ready to take on more responsibilities. She pointed out that, unlike other buyers at her level, she had experience supervising ten staff in her previous job, and that this equipped her with the skills to take on a supervisory role.

Jennifer's employer realized that her combination of new skills and previous experience were valuable enough to land her a job elsewhere for a much larger salary. They had also been impressed with the long hours and hard work Jennifer had put in over those two years and they didn't want to lose her. Jennifer's employer offered her a position as a merchandise manager for the Western region, the kind of job she had been working towards since the day she walked out of the insurance office.

*The Glitter Factor*

The toughest part of accepting a stepping-stone job is that it usually involves a "step down" for people — a necessary descent into the valley for a temporary period to equip oneself for the eventual climb up to the summit of the ultimate career target. For this reason, these jobs can be difficult to bear. It is important to remind yourself that the slog to get to higher ground is both temporary and neccesary. To sweeten an otherwise unpalatable stepping- stone job, try to look for a position that offers some glamorous aspects.

After three years at a prestigious law firm, I wanted to go back into management. That meant a mid-level role, which might seem a step down from being a lawyer. But because I wanted a bit of glamour, I chose a new career in the airline industry. It offered perks like free flights (whenever there were open seats) anywhere in the world.

In my five years with the airline, I had three entirely different jobs. The least glamorous was a two-year stint running the Customer Relations (read "Complaint") Department. This department was in dreadful shape and needed someone who could cut costs and dramatically improve performance — a tall order, but something an aspiring young manager needs to learn. Here was a hands-on opportunity that would give me operational management experience. Like bad medicine, I knew this was a work experience I should have. It was a true stepping-stone job.

I had fifty staff members, primarily unionized workers. I had an interior office in an industrial park, my view of the mountains from my former law office only a hazy memory. My salary was $25,000 less a year than I had been earning.

When I would attend events with my former law school classmates it was sometimes hard to hold my head high. I found myself face-to-face with my evident loss of status. The fact that I considered myself to be on my way to bigger and better things was small consolation. What helped most through that dark period was the "glitter factor" associated with my job, which allowed me to chime in as they discussed the purchase of their new sports cars and condos: "I've just been to Paris for the weekend!"

Rightly or wrongly, it made me feel a little bit better about where my career was at that moment. Many years later I came to feel a *lot* better about where my career was at relative to theirs. When I entered into my final career target, the glitter came not from any glamorous perks but from the nature of the work itself. I was earning enough to buy my own sports car and travel around the world without needing free passes. But during those dog days of a stepping-stone job, the "glitter factor" helped me through the valley, like a sugar coating on a bad-tasting pill.

## The Fuzzy Womb of Academia

As you deliberate on your job targets, you may also consider going back to school. The desire to return to the fuzzy womb of academia only to be "reborn" again into a brighter career is a strong temptation. But it can also be a lengthy and expensive process. An MBA, for example, is generally two years of full-time work or roughly five years of part-time. There will be program expenses and foregone income to consider. Even going part-time means some career decisions may have to wait (such as a transfer or temporary assignments in another city) while your program is under way. Consider carefully whether you really *need* to go back to school in order to step onto the career path that you desire. If not, you may be better investing that time gaining work experience in a stepping-stone job.

In my executive compensation practice, for example, most people have MBAs or law degrees. But one very successful practitioner has a Bachelor of Commerce and experience in human resource management. She considered returning to school for an MBA and then found she could convince our firm to hire her without it. She is now two years further ahead in her career than she would have been had she gone back to school.

By all means do *not* go back to school and invest time, money, and effort without first identifying and plotting out a career path. Those who don't are often lost when the program ends. That doesn't mean you can't change your mind as you go through the program. You may find other possibilities open up that previously held no interest or with which you were previously unfamiliar. But you will be further ahead if you have some sort of plan (albeit subject to possible change) before making the major investment that going back to school requires.

If you decide school is the only way to reach your career goals, consider how the program itself might help you make valuable contacts in your chosen field. Don't wait for graduation to start this process. Get in touch with the company you'd most like to work for on graduation right away, and see if you can do some projects with them as part of your course of study. This was a strategy that worked well for me when I did my own MBA. Before even beginning the program, I approached the employer I wanted to work for and asked them about doing my thesis on a subject that interested them. They suggested I use their company as a "case study" in applying my thesis. This enabled me to study the organization at minimal cost to them. I met people at all levels of the organization and learned much about the corporate culture.

Because I was keen to impress them, I worked hard and tried to ensure that my work would be of value to them. My preliminary work led them to create a position for me before graduation, and they agreed to pay for my MBA as I continued on a part-time basis. Even more important, the insights I had gained through studying their company as a student were a huge benefit as I began the new job.

While I always felt very fortunate about how this study arrangement worked out, I have often heard employers comment that they would be receptive to these sorts of proposals from students. Most employers relish the chance to get "free" assistance from the outside. Besides, the arrangement provides a relatively risk-free environment that gives the student exposure to the organization and its people, while exposing the organization to the student's capabilities and interests.

Students often rely upon the school to provide access to future employers rather than taking their own initiative. But competition increases when the entire class is clamouring for attention from the one or two prospective employers the school has brought in for a study project. If *you* bring the project in, it is all yours. Not only is there no competition but the employer is generally impressed with the initiative you have taken in seeking them out for a study project so closely aligned with their own needs. It speaks volumes in your favour.

So, if at the end of your deliberations you decide that a semester or more of hitting the books is a necessary step on your career path, go a little further and consider who your dream employer might be at the end of the path. And how you might engage them at the outset. This will undoubtedly give you a better chance of learning about them and securing a position with them (if you still want it after what you may learn about them!) when you are finished your program.

The other reason to try to do some of this while in school is that it enables you to develop your networking skills before you actually have to use them to find a job at the completion of your degree or course. The basic techniques for networking your way to an academic project with a prospective employer are almost exactly the same as those described in later chapters for networking your way to a new career/job. The only major difference is that academic projects allow for more cold-calling and less time spent establishing credentials.

## *Textbooks for Job Targets 101*

As you prepare for your first weekend in seclusion to define your job targets, you should consider bringing with you some resource materials that can help to guide you through the three dimensions you will be working on. An hour or so at your local library or bookstore will yield fruitful results on all these topics. All the same, you must keep focussed. Resist bringing along mountains of materials that you will never be able to get through in one weekend. Listed below are three of the most helpful resource materials you can use for each of the three areas you'll be thinking about.

— **Money Goals**: *Think and Grow Rich* by Napoleon Hill
This book is a classic. While some will find it dated, I believe it is still a gem. It provides a thorough rationale for setting monetary goals and discusses this process in detail. Readers will easily see how its approach can be applied to career targeting.
— **Passions/Interests**: *Wishcraft: How to Get What You Really Want* by Barbara Sher
This book contains plenty of exercises to help readers identify their passions and interests. It is particularly helpful for those feeling "blocked" and looking to uncover areas of interest that they haven't been able to find on their own.
— **Transferable Skills**: *What Color is your Parachute?* by Richard Bolles
This classic guide for the traditional job hunter has an excellent section on transferable skills and some useful exercises

(particularly in the Appendices) to help you identify which of these transferable skills you most want to use in your job targets.

## The Outcome: Not One, Not Two, but Three Job Targets

The outcome of the process should be to identify not one, not two, but *three* job targets, all of which would meet or come close to meeting the criteria of the three questions explored. These should be prioritized as Job Targets A, B, and C in order of your preference. Target A would be your first choice, the one that seems closest to reaching your monetary goals, tapping into your strongest passions, and using your talents and skills to maximum advantage. Targets B and C should be relatively different types of career targets. That means they should not simply be doing the same type of job as Target A with another organization or in another venue, such as Director of New Business Development at ABC Company, DEF Company, and XYZ Company. They should each involve an entirely different set of employers. The less overlap the better; it produces a broader range of options for you. If Target A is in an industry that unfortunately has fallen on hard times, Target B is likely to hold more possibilities.

During my last career change, I developed three very different job targets. The first was an area I called "corporate governance consulting." If you've never heard of this area, you're not alone — I hadn't either. The job, as I envisioned it, involved providing advice to the boards of companies about executive and director pay, board and CEO effectiveness, and other issues relating to how boards govern corporations. This interest arose out of the experience I had working with a coalition of unions to save the airline I was then working for from bankruptcy. My interest in this area was supplemented by some work I had done in a stepping-stone job involving executive compensation and corporate governance issues from a legal perspective. So here was Job Target A.

The second was in an area I called "government relations consulting." I had no background in political science or government relations, but as part of this same earlier experience I had been responsible for briefing teams of employees to meet with their local politicians about legal issues relating to our company. This lobbying had been interesting and satisfying work from my perspective. While I had no interest in becoming a lobbyist in the traditional sense of the word, I felt that my experience here might be very useful to other corporations who wanted to involve their workforces as part of their strategy to deal with political issues. So here was Job Target B.

Finally, I had an interest in returning to a role in operational management but wasn't sure of an appropriate entry point. Nothing stood out on the passions/interest side, nor did a particular industry tickle my fancy. I decided to fall back on transferable skills and use my experience as a lawyer as the way in. So Job Target C became a corporate counsel position, from which I hoped to transport myself back over to the management side once I had uncovered an interesting opportunity.

It's difficult enough to come up with one job target, you argue, so why develop *three*? As discussed earlier, having one be-all-and-end-all job target simply creates too much pressure, that stranded feeling that if it doesn't pan out, it seems as if there are no other options. And it's easy to make unnecessary compromises in achieving that job target if you have not taken the time to develop a range of alternatives. It is almost always worth the additional effort to place yourself in a less vulnerable position by broadening your options.

Having three job targets also provides you with a "safety hatch." If you are ultimately dissatisfied with your choice after you've accepted a new job, it becomes much easier to face the prospect of moving in a different direction if you have explored other alternatives in the course of your career change. You may, in fact, already have the contacts necessary to make another change quickly and painlessly.

## "Help! My Dream Job Is Something No One Has Ever Heard Of!"

If you go through the process of developing job targets based on your passions and your transferable skills, chances are that you may arrive at one that seems "perfect" for you but which you have never heard of before. While there is often a tendency to panic when this occurs, it may really be time to shout "Eureka!" To determine whether this is the case, ask yourself some of the following questions:

— How would this job/service/product be of value to someone?
— To whom would this service/product be most valuable?
— How much money would a "customer" be likely to pay for this service/product?
— What are the names of organizations that would currently be selling services/products to these types of "customers" or might have people employed in positions that provide somewhat similar or complementary services/products?
— Would this "job" most readily lend itself to a specific industry or would the service/product be useful in a number of industries?
— Does this "job" lend itself most readily to full- or part-time employment or to a contract where the service/product is "sold" to numerous customers? Which of these scenarios best suits my employment needs?

If, after considering some of these issues, it becomes apparent that you have arrived at a job that would provide enough value to a customer or employer to yield you the level of income you are looking for, you have a winner! Don't hesitate for a moment to include this among your job targets.

There are some tremendous benefits in arriving at a "new job" no one has heard of before. First off, there may be virtually no competition in the field. It gives you an opportunity to establish yourself as an "expert" in short order once you move into an employment situation in this new area. Second, you will probably not meet the frustrating response of "We already have someone here doing that job" when you approach prospective employers. Finally, and most important, unlike a traditional job, you have a better understanding than anyone of exactly what this job would involve and how it would be of value. The key is to convey that expertise to a prospective employer or "customer."

You may have to be even more thorough in your research than someone targeting a traditional position. You will have to define the job so that it has an authentic ring and does not sound like some "pie-in-the-sky" notion hazily developed over a few beers in the backyard after a bad day at work. And you need to be ready to demonstrate exactly how this job can make a significant contribution to an organization, or that there would be a market for the service or product this job would provide.

Previously unheard-of jobs are not without attendant pitfalls even after you have convinced a prospective employer to give you a shot at creating this new position within their organization. Because it is something new, employers will often have difficulty determining where to position the job within an existing organization. Therefore, you need to have a fairly definite idea about the kind of income this job should be capable of producing. Otherwise, you may be willing to settle for a conservative salary just for the opportunity to try it out.

If the employer offers you the job at a modest initial salary until you prove your value, you might want to consider it as a stepping-stone job that will ultimately lead to a more satisfactory pay arrangement. But if you feel that your current skills are sufficiently well developed even in this relatively new field, you should continue your search until you find an employer willing to pay you full value for this new job.

Regardless of the pay, you will also face considerably more pressure to prove the value of the job early on. The employer will probably be looking to see some tangible return on investment, be it in the form of new clients, cost savings, or a significant new piece of business or revenue, and they will expect it within twelve to eighteen months of your coming on board. If you decide to tackle the new job on a contract basis, you may be forced to withstand the financial costs of a start-up phase on your own.

While your immediate reaction may be: "Yikes! Who needs that pressure?" stop and consider for a moment that *you* also need to be convinced that there is value in the new job you have created. If after twelve to eighteen months the new job is not yielding fruit, perhaps it is time to reconsider whether it is worth devoting more time to this endeavour. Perhaps you will take the lessons you have learned from trying it out and formulate a new career strategy. Remember that nothing is ever a complete loss. A savvy career entrepreneur learns to build on the skills and experience gained even in an ultimately unsuccessful venture.

If the new job is a winner, however, and the world is beating a path to your door, you may be able to command a premium for your skills. In this situation, you are likely to experience an extremely high level of career satisfaction — the very thing you were looking for when you set about making the change. Perhaps more important, you will realize that if this exciting new field someday loses its lustre, you are now a veteran of the process of creating a career for yourself in a completely new area — and you can do it again if you ever want or need to.

# *Tools of the Career-Changing Trade*

An artist can't paint without brushes. A plumber can't unplug drains without a plunger. And a career changer/job hunter can't get very far without a tool kit for this particular "line of work." The good news is that *your* basic tool kit is sure to be less costly than that of nearly any other profession or trade, and probably only slightly more than an ice cream sundae. The kit should include:

- one $1.99 scribbler that will be your networking notebook;
- one floppy disk on which to keep three versions of your résumé; and
- one library card.

You will notice that a computer and printer are *not* on the list. I have not included them because most of you probably have access to a computer and printer at virtually no charge — namely, the one in your current workplace. The home computer of a good friend or family member may be another option, provided you have ongoing access and a good printer.

If neither of these pan out, there are businesses that allow pay-by-the-hour access or monthly rental services. Public libraries and employment centres often offer free access to computers and the Internet. These may be just the thing if you have security concerns about your workplace computer. They also prevent you from having to keep odd hours at the office just to ensure privacy.

## *The Networking Notebook*

Things get lost. That's just the way it is. Consider the following items you might easily lose:

— The back of the envelope where you scribbled down the name of two contacts at Grade A Corporation provided to you by your squash buddy over lunch.
— The torn-out page on which you prepared a To Do list of things for the job hunt last week, that you had hidden away in a briefcase, pocket, or purse. You know that the fourth item on that list was something quite important but you haven't done it yet and you can't find the page with the list to refresh your memory.
— The business card of the vice-president from Grade B Corporation whom you met at a Board of Trade reception three weeks ago.

When we are in the midst of the career-change or job-hunt process, we are often hasty to "dispose of the evidence," particularly if we are currently employed. Yet, as we gather more information along the way and our priorities shift in response to new information, items that seemed unimportant one week may take on greater significance the next. It is Murphy's Law that the speed at which items tend to get lost in the career-change process are inversely proportionate to the items' relative importance to us. For example, it is only after we realize that Grade B Corporation (which we were viewing with only passing interest up until today) is really the workplace of our dreams that we will suddenly find we cannot locate the business card from the vice-president and we can't remember that person's name and department.

So we need a place to keep everything together. Someplace where all contact names will be written down — and never ripped out or crossed off beyond recognition. A place to write down all our To Do lists and never throw them out even after most items have been tackled — it is often that one "untackled" item that we are inevitably searching to remind ourselves about. A place to keep notes from our brainstorming, our library research, and our research through networking — so that they are all together in one place, saving us time hunting through desk drawers and brief-cases every time we need to refer to them.

You can avoid these mishaps by keeping everything related to your job search in a networking notebook. An ordinary lined coil scribbler will do. It is less tempting to remove and insert pages, and coil scribblers are light and portable. There are several computer programs on the market that can provide you with an electronic version of a networking notebook. If that's what works best for you, go get one. The format you use isn't as important as the time and energy you put into the research and ideas that fill up the notebook.

Your networking notebook should be purchased even before you begin your job target deliberations. You might even consider using it to write out your brainstorming ideas. These notes may help you later on. For example, you may wonder exactly why you chose a particular job target. Or perhaps there was a fourth job target that you developed but dismissed when you were paring it down to three, but you now need to use it as a replacement. Whatever the target is, the networking notebook ensures that it will all be right there at your fingertips.

## The First Entries in Your Networking Notebook

Whether or not you use your notebook as part of setting job targets, one of the first entries after that process has been completed should be the following:

— A list of Job Targets A, B, and C with a short description of each in order to capture the essence of the job target.

— A To Do list consisting of a minimum of five, and a maximum of twenty, tasks you will need to do to get your job hunt under way. The list should incorporate some of the research and networking ideas set out in the later chapters of this book.

Here is an example:

### Job Targets

**Target A:** Associate Editor: Travel, Leisure, Arts and Lifestyle sections of local newspaper. Editor with final decision-making authority over all articles published in these sections, including authority over format, content, layout, etc. Occasionally acts as contributing writer in these sections.

**Target B:** Freelance Travel Writer: Regular contributor to national and international magazines such as *Gourmet*, *Condé Nast Traveler*, and others.

**Target C:** Creative Writing Professor/Instructor at College Level: Teaches full course load of creative writing and journalism at one of three local colleges/vocational schools in the local area.

### To Do List

1. Phone Caroline M., close friend of editor-in-chief of one of the local papers for coffee to find out current happenings at local paper, possibility of meeting editor-in-chief for coffee.

2. Go to library and review back issues of *Gourmet*, etc., to obtain names of editors and review types of articles.

3. Contact magazine editors found in (2) to investigate types of articles each will buy (preferred length, with or without accompanying photos, North American or international locations preferred, etc.) and process for submitting proposals/articles.

4. Phone Kyle C., former classmate from journalism program who became editor of the Arts and Leisure section of the *Chicago Tribune* to discuss likes/dislikes of position, my credentials to work in this field, his contacts in my city, etc.

5. Go to Merrymont College, and obtain current curriculum for English/Journalism program and list of faculty.

6. Call my friend Trent W., instructor of mechanical engineering at Merrymont College, to find out more about Merrymont and who I should contact in English/Journalism faculty to explore possibilities.

7. Phone Elizabeth D., my old journalism professor who used to be a staff writer at *National Geographic*, to discuss pros/cons of freelance work for major magazines and potential contacts in my areas of interest. Ask if she would be willing to act as one of my references.

### How to Use To Do Lists to Overcome Setbacks in the Job Hunt

To Do lists should be written in the networking notebook and *not* ripped out, even if all the items are eventually crossed off the list. My hunch is that a few of the items are unlikely to get crossed off the list in the first instance, anyway. What generally happens is that you start working your way down the list — calling up Caroline for coffee, getting over to the library to look at the magazines, running into Trent at the grocery store — and before you know it, things start to happen!

Caroline has arranged a lunch for you and the editor-in-chief. Trent informs you that the journalism department at Merrymont just lost an instructor who transferred to Nebraska. He knows the dean and suggests you give him a call, using Trent's name. And suddenly it looks as if some of your job targets are about to break! You quickly abandon the remainder of the list and focus on these interesting "leads."

And then what happens?

You meet with the editor-in-chief and find out that Larry Q. has been the associate editor of Arts and Leisure at that paper for several hundred years and there doesn't seem to be much possibility of making inroads there, even for someone (like yourself) with excellent credentials. The only job at that paper would be to work for Larry. It would be a stepping-stone position and is only likely to transform itself into your dream job if Larry gets hit by a bus. While not a complete washout, it doesn't look promising.

You use Trent's name and call the dean at Merrymont, inviting him for coffee. You discover that a selection committee is already in the middle of second interviews with three candidates to replace the instructor who has left for Nebraska. Although he seems impressed with your credentials and enthusiasm, he feels it is simply too late to throw another candidate's name into the ring for this job.

So then what do you do? If you're human, you'll probably respond the way most of us would and get discouraged. What seemed to be promising leads have turned to dust! *But*, if you have been clever enough to save your original To Do list in your networking notebook, you will have just the thing to kick-start your job hunt by falling back on the items that have *not* yet been tackled. After taking time to regroup, you can place your calls to Kyle and Elizabeth as well as to the editors of some of those magazines in the library. And before you know it, new leads will emerge again. Perhaps these too will result in some dead-ends, but eventually they will begin to yield serious possibilities. Returning to your networking notebook when new ideas are needed will not only save you a lot of time and energy but will keep you from losing momentum.

### *Using the Networking Notebook for Its Main Purpose*

While using the networking notebook to keep To Do lists can serve a valuable purpose, its primary function is to keep networking information. This data generally falls into the following categories:

- Information about people you should contact, developed from your networking. This information would include name, phone and fax numbers, and any special interests or common ground you may have with the contact (alumni from same college, used to work in your current occupation and has made the same type of career change you are considering, etc.).
- Notes from your library research. (To be discussed later in this chapter.)

Finally, if you do end up answering some career advertisements or making contact with headhunters in addition to your jumping-ship efforts, make sure you paste copies of those ads into your networking notebook, along with information about any headhunters you speak with — their names, and phone and fax numbers. While it is my view that both of these methods generally yield less satisfactory results when making a career change than the process outlined for jumping ship, I would never discourage anyone from responding to an interesting career ad, or talking to a headhunter at the same time.

Your networking notebook should provide one handy, compact

place where you can find absolutely *everything* relating to your job search, and you should work with it on a daily basis throughout your job hunt. Refer to your To Do lists and update them without ripping out the old ones. Add in other thoughts about contacts or comments from meetings with people you've contacted. At all times, resist the temptation to "clean up" the notebook by throwing out information. If the book is becoming too full, buy a new one! Keep old ones in a very safe place; you will refer to them many times throughout the job hunt. And remember to keep your networking notebook long after you find a new job. It will be your insurance policy should things not work out. It holds other ideas, leads, information, and contacts that might prove to be invaluable if you decide to jump ship yet again.

## There's No Such Thing as a One-Size-Fits-All Résumé

Computerization has relegated one-size-fits-all résumés to the dustbins of history. It is now possible to tailor résumés to a specific job target with very minimal time and effort. Different aspects of your experience can be emphasized for different job targets. You may, for example, include a summer workshop on a particular topic or a transferable skill in a résumé tailored towards Job Target A without including it in a résumé for Job Target B. The following example illustrates how you would highlight different skills and experiences for different job targets.

### Job Targets

**Target A:** Associate Editor, Travel, Arts and Leisure
The résumé should emphasize experience and training as an editor, any experience working on a major daily newspaper

that demonstrates ability to cope with daily deadlines, etc., as well as experience in the travel, arts, and leisure sectors either as a writer or in some other capacity that would demonstrate working knowledge of these areas.

**Target B:** Freelance Travel Writer

This may be a field where a résumé is not usually required — proposals for articles or actual articles may be all that are generally considered. Nonetheless, developing a résumé for this job target may prove a useful exercise. This résumé should emphasize experience as a travel writer and should also outline published freelance articles and list places travelled to, so as to assure the reader that this is a sophisticated traveller as well as an experienced writer.

**Target C:** Creative Writing Instructor

The résumé should emphasize both teaching experience and experience in the field of creative writing as a published writer of books, articles, or other journalistic forms. As this résumé will be targeted to academic institutions, academic credentials will be of increased importance and should be highlighted.

Creating three versions of your résumé *at the outset* allows you to provide a résumé tailored to each job target on a moment's notice. As you progress in your research, you may create even more versions of your résumé, tailored to "sub-sets" of the job targets. For example, if you decide to pursue positions as an instructor of both creative writing and of journalism, two similar but different résumés should be prepared. Both would emphasize teaching but one would focus on creative writing skills and experience, while the other would highlight journalism experience.

As soon as you have developed job targets and tailored your résumés accordingly, make sure you copy all versions onto a floppy disk so you can print them off whenever they may be required.

## *Résumé Lore*

There are literally hundreds of books and articles written on the subject of résumés. I suggest you thumb through a handful of them at your local library to look for useful ideas. In the process, you will notice that there is a great deal of "résumé lore." Some sources will advise you to keep your résumé to one page in length. Others will urge you to elaborate on your experience and accomplishments in your prior work — even if it ends up running to three pages. Some will suggest including a photograph; others will strongly advise against this practice.

Styles and structures of résumés will also vary. Some use a chronological format. Others highlight relevant skills at the outset. Either will do, in my opinion, as long as the reader clearly understands what it is in your background that makes you well suited to your targeted position. *That* is the overall objective of the résumé, and the means to that end can likely be accomplished in as many ways as there are books on the subject.

Find one or two trusted friends, preferably with some degree of sophistication in the target field, to take a look at your draft résumés and offer comments. If your reviewer is someone who knows you well, he or she may even be able to offer suggestions about your skills and experience that you might have forgotten. Remember also that everyone who reviews your résumés will have their own pet peeves and preferences. I personally dislike listing hobbies and interests at the end of the résumé because whatever you do in your spare time is not really my concern unless it has direct relevance to the position in question. But other people really like that little section because they believe it gives them a greater sense of the "whole person." There's no right answer, so incorporate only those suggestions that strike you as making a substantive improvement to your initial drafts.

## How the Role of the Résumé Differs for Those Who Are Jumping Ship

While the résumé is an essential tool for changing careers and jobs, its importance must be viewed in context. If you are relying heavily on newspaper or Internet advertisements, the résumé increases in importance. It becomes the *only* tool you have to convince a prospective employer to give you an interview.

If you are jumping ship, however, the résumé plays a different role. Phone calls and meetings take precedence. These activities, and not the résumé, become the door-opener. The résumé serves largely to provide written reinforcement of information you have conveyed orally. It will likely be passed on to others after an initial meeting, but with a certain degree of editorializing on the part of the person you have spoken with and given the résumé to. Their comments will colour how your résumé will be viewed by the recipient.

For those who are jumping ship, other aspects of the career-change process (such as researching and networking) are often more important than the résumé in securing the position you are after. For the currently employed, who have limited time to spend on job-seeking activities each week, this is an important consideration; keep it in mind as you budget time for résumé preparation.

## Your Librarian: More Valuable Than a Headhunter

"Research" is a term that gets a bum rap. It evokes images of librarians clad in cat's-eye glasses or men in white lab coats with pocket protectors. But however tedious the idea may seem, public, university, and college libraries are teeming with exactly the information you need to begin making real progress in your job search. They are a resource you can't afford to ignore, and they cost you nothing but some time and effort. They are also filled with kindly people (not all of whom wear cat's-eye glasses) who are generally more than happy to help you find what you need.

"Research" should also include some Internet time. If you're not currently online there are plenty of pay-as-you-play services available, with equally friendly people on hand to provide assistance. While the cost may be as much as $20 per hour, the information you have access to is massive. Three or four hours on the Net may seem pricey but the cost is often less than couriering three résumés to answer newspaper ads.

What are you looking for in these libraries and on the Internet? The one thing you are *not* looking for is job postings. You are looking for information about the fields you have identified as Job Targets A, B, and C — information that will allow you to determine whether there is potential for you to move into this area and prospective employers who might hire you. Make sure you note whether these organizations have been involved in interesting new activities in the field, how they are doing financially, and the names of potential contacts. You might also consult the following sources for information of this kind.

— *Journal articles about the field*. The more specific the journal, the better your ability to learn more and carry on an intelligent conversation with people in the field. The more you learn about trends in your chosen field, the more ideas you should develop about finding your way in. Note the names of people and organizations who have authored some of the better articles — they are prime candidates for networking. Looking at the authors and where they are employed will also give you fresh ideas about organizations that employ people in this area — possibly potential employers you were unfamiliar with before.

— *Directories*. There are general directories that list companies or organizations. See, for instance, the *Wall Street Journal 350*, *Financial Post* sectoral directories, and books or magazine articles that list the best companies to work for. Other directories exist for specific fields. Lawyers, for example, use the *Martindale-Hubbell Directory*, which provides specific information on both law firms and lawyers. You can find information such as the name of the person who is the head of the real estate department or the corporate finance group at a law firm that interests you. *Martindale-Hubbell* goes further to provide personal backgrounds for the lawyers listed. If you find a lawyer at a firm that interests you who went to the same law school you did, or with whom you share something else in common, be sure to write it down. Having something in common makes it easier to build rapport when you contact this person. Be sure to consult your librarian to make sure you know of *all* the directories relating to your field before you head for home.

— *Newspapers/magazines.* Like trade journals, local or national newspapers and magazines may also carry articles relating to either your field of interest or companies that might hire for the sort of position you have targeted. These articles often quote experts in the field and give some details about where they work. Make sure you write down these experts' names and any information that might allow you to contact them. Fight the temptation to trawl through the careers section.

— *Annual reports.* Many libraries — particularly those at universities or colleges — have extensive collections of company annual reports. If Companies X, Y, and Z are of interest to you, find their annual reports and thumb through them. Annual reports are a wealth of information. The nature of the company's business, sometimes including a summary of the very department that interests you, will help you decide if their activities capture your imagination. Senior management are often identified as well. Perhaps most important, you can gauge how the company is doing financially. If it is constantly in the red, and things are getting worse, it may be best to look elsewhere — unless your interest is in insolvency! If, however, they're growing by leaps and bounds, and your area of interest seems to be contributing to that growth, chances are they may want to talk to *you* even more than you want to see them!

— *Web sites.* Company web sites provide excellent information at your fingertips, and typically include access to financial information. Research of journals, articles, and even directories can also be conducted online and, in many cases, will be faster and smoother for you than a trip to the library. Take time to print off or write down the names of authors and experts quoted in articles and try to tape or staple print-outs into your networking notebook so they are not lost in the future. Again, try to resist the job bulletin boards for now, and focus on your research.

## *What to Do with Your Library Research*

By the end of your first trip to the library or your first surf around the Net, your networking notebook should be starting to take shape with names, ideas, and other information. It is now time to try to synthesize this into a second To Do list of steps you need to take to proceed with your job search. If all went well, your research should have helped you to identify organizations of interest and, ideally, contact names.

After some solid research, you may want to step back for a moment and consider the priority of your job targets. These may change as you find out more about your field of interest and possible contacts. You may discover, for example, that Job Target B (initially your second choice) actually has much greater potential than you first thought, moving it up to top priority. Alternatively, you may discover a new job target you had not previously considered. You may wish to replace one of your initial choices or simply add this new discovery as a fourth target. Be careful, however, not to let your list grow too much longer than four job targets. You don't want to divide your energies and spread your resources too thin.

Bear in mind that the research phase is not a one-shot deal. While a solid weekend of work generally equips you to move into the next phase of networking, you should continue to devote time to research throughout the process. This will help you maintain fresh ideas and leads, as well as make you increasingly knowledgeable about your job target and trends in the field. If you can, try to spend one to two hours on research every weekend throughout the duration of your job search.

# *Six Degrees of Separation*

Now that you've immersed yourself long enough in the library or on the Web to feel more aware of what's going on in your field of interest, and once you have compiled a list of prospects, it's time to move on to the networking phase of the research process. I almost hesitate to use the word "networking," given the negative and insincere connotations associated with it. Networking conjures up images of shallow people having superficial conversations while buttering croissants.

Networking, however, means nothing more than getting out and meeting people. When you're in the middle of a career change or job hunt, there are two important kinds of people to meet:

— people who can provide you with insights about your targeted line of work and suggest possible contacts; and
— people who can hire you.

John Guare's play, *Six Degrees of Separation*, and the movie of the same name were based on the premise that everyone on the planet is connected to everyone else by only six other people: "From the President of the United States to a gondolier in Venice. And not just big names," muses Guare's character Ouisa. "It's anyone. A native in a rain forest to an Eskimo. I am bound to everyone on this planet by a trail of six people. But you have to find the right six people to make the connection."

I have no idea if there's any scientific basis for this premise, but in my experience the trail to finding the people who may hire you is generally a lot fewer than six. It often constitutes fewer than four people. Nonetheless, you still have to find the *right* four people to make the right connection. Remember: *Somebody knows somebody who knows somebody who knows the person you want to meet.*

## *Nearly Everybody May Be A Somebody*

Who *are* the people you should be networking with as you set out to change your career and find an exciting new job? I once read an article that suggested: "Network with everyone you have ever met in your entire life." Do I agree with that? Well, almost. If you are still employed, your current boss and the majority of your coworkers are probably out. Apart from that, I use the following litmus test: *If the person you are thinking of calling and asking for contacts or other help in considering a career change called you and asked you the same question, would you help him or her? If the answer is yes, give that person a call.*

To get you started, here are some ideas about where to begin networking:

— *People you went to school with.* Generally, college or university friends are a good bet, but don't forget high school friends or even people you know from courses at night school, seminars in your field, etc. If you graduated within the last five to seven years, don't forget professors or teachers — they probably haven't forgotten you!

— *People you used to work with.* These could be coworkers or bosses from a previous job or they could be people who used to work at the company where you are currently employed. Those who have left jobs at your current workplace are often the most helpful networking contacts as they are often keen to help someone else follow a similar path. If they have made a career shift in the same direction you are considering, even better. They will be a wealth of information about the transition and will probably be able to provide a great deal of insight as well as wonderful contacts. The only cautionary note to consider is whether you feel confident that they will keep your intentions under wraps if they maintain close friendships with your current boss and coworkers.

— *People in your field who work elsewhere.* This refers to colleagues at other companies or organizations who you have met either through working together or through professional associations and gatherings. Bankers, for example, often tend to know their colleagues at other banks. Again, try to ensure that the person you approach is not a close friend of your current boss or coworkers.

— *People you know socially.* Friends; your spouse's friends; friends of friends whom you've met at parties, weddings, and other social events; people from your hockey team or golf club; people you met working on a political campaign or volunteering at the food bank; neighbours; people from your Block Watch or condominium committee; parents of your children's friends or classmates; the person sitting next to you on a three-hour flight to Dallas — there's no limit to whom you might approach.

— *People you know who provide personal services.* Your hairdresser, broker, doctor, lawyer, squash instructor, or personal trainer.

All of these people come into contact with folks from all walks of life — perhaps from the very field or company that interests you. While this may sound a little off-beat, don't underestimate it.

— *Family.* Blood is thicker than water and when it comes to job hunting, you'd be amazed how helpful family connections can turn out to be. You might be reluctant to use them because it involves divulging your plans for a career change — possibly to an unreceptive audience who will spend more time protesting the idea than offering contacts. After all, if you approach your father, who helped pay your way through law school, to advise him that you want to be a screenwriter instead and ask if he has any contacts, you can probably expect his reply to be something other than a list of the names and phone numbers of his screenwriter pals! There are definite downsides to family networking, but there are upsides, too. Assess the risks and benefits and, if the benefits seem greater, give it a go.

What exactly do you say to these contacts when you do call them for assistance? What do you say to Linda, your former classmate, or Fred, with whom you used to work, or Karl from your health club? You need to tailor your approach to your own personal style, but here are a couple of suggestions.

**Approach A:** "I've been the head of marketing at my company for four years now, but recently I've developed an interest in corporate finance. I know that sounds like quite a switch — and it is — but it's something I got a taste for last year when our company went public, and the field has captured my interest ever since. Going into corporate finance would be a big switch for me and I really want to do my homework before I make any decisions about that. Because you're a corporate lawyer who takes companies public, I was wondering if you knew any investment bankers who might be willing to talk with me about this field and give me some insight. I'd also be interested in your perspective."

**Approach B**: "I've been the head of marketing at my company for four years now. A few months ago, I started following some of the things going on at Millennium Industries, and I got really interested in their acquisition of a little software design house that was doing some really creative stuff. I'd love to talk with some people at Millennium to find out more about them. You mentioned something about having Millennium do some work for your company last year and I was wondering if you could suggest the name of someone I might speak with there."

Both approaches use the context of research as a way of getting contact names. *Never* say that you are looking for a job. *Always* say that you are "thinking about making a career move and want to find out more information before making a decision." This isn't being dishonest because your priority at this stage of the game is information gathering. If it just so happens that you have a terrific meeting with someone at Millennium Industries that leads to a job offer in record time, then it's a case of serendipity! You may decide to make a career move. But until that time you are still researching. You may well discover that your job target A is less than the bed of roses you thought it would be. You could meet the president of Millennium Industries and decide that he is a direct descendant of Attila the Hun and his little software design house is losing people faster than the deck of the *Titanic*. Before you know it, this job target is struck off your list! Won't you be glad that you never told anyone you were looking for a job in that field?

You also need to give your friends and contacts some credit. They are not naïve. They know that anyone who is asking these kinds of questions is looking at a change pretty seriously. Chances are, they've done something similar themselves. And if they have, they can appreciate that you have to do a fair amount of digging before you make any decisions. They should respect the fact that you want to do your homework before becoming doe-eyed over a prospective new position. In fact, they are likely to respect you far more than if you said, "Yes, I'm looking to make a move into corporate finance. Haven't met anybody in the field, haven't talked to any prospective employers, but, yessireee, I'm looking for a job in corporate finance!"

Be sure you jot down all contact names, phone numbers, and any other relevant information in your networking notebook shortly after the call or the meeting so you can refer to it again. Include the name of the person who provided the contact right beside it, as well as any other pertinent details while they are fresh in your mind. This might include, for example, that Jane Doe at the XYZ Company also went to your university. Last, and most important, ask your friend or acquaintance if you may use their name when you call. This is a critical component in turning what would otherwise be a "cold call" into a "warm call."

## Brainstorming Parties

One of the more unconventional ideas to help jump-start the networking process is to hold a brainstorming party. While it may not be for everyone, it has been known to yield worthwhile results. Here's how it works: Rather than calling up each of your friends individually and asking if they knew anyone at Hardball Capital, you invite them all over for a brainstorming party at your place. Anywhere from ten to twenty people will do; more than that might be a bit unworkable. If you have forty friends that you think could help out, hold two parties!

Once everyone has a drink in hand, stand up, gather them all around, and tell them the reason for the party. Explain that you have decided to explore some new career opportunities and would like their help in making contact with some people in the new fields you're considering. Tell them your three job targets and, without going into great depth, give them some idea of why you are interested in each area. Then outline the elements of your background that may be well suited to each job target.

Turn it into a game by taking each job target in turn and asking your guests whether they know the names of potential employers, or anyone who works in the area. You might consider getting paper and an easel to write down responses. Keep the pages or notes that come out of this party — they may be worth much more than what you spent on the drinks and nibbles.

The key to making the brainstorming party a success is to get your guests to come up with contact names. A few cautionary notes:

- Don't let your guests engage you in a lengthy debate about the wisdom of your job target choices. If they have concerns, simply tell them that "No job is perfect, and I realize there are probably some pitfalls with this one, too. But I've done a lot of thinking about this and would like to explore it further."
- Resist the temptation to get into a down-and-dirty discussion about all the things that are bothering you about your current job. It may feel good to describe your present frustration in a room full of friends, but this will take time away from your goal of generating contacts. The tenor of the evening may change as guests follow suit by launching into their own frustrations with *their* jobs. While this may make for an interesting evening, it does not fulfill the purpose for which you bought the wine.

Holding a brainstorming party can be particularly useful for someone who is either not currently working or is trying to re-enter the workforce after time away. It will serve to rally friends and help you communicate to them that you are serious about finding a new job. Not only are they likely to come up with some excellent contact ideas, but you can expect to receive calls with other suggestions, long after the party has ended.

Don't hold a brainstorming party if a number of the invitees know people at your present workplace. This might make them think you are being open about your plans, and they may not treat the issue with the same degree of secrecy they would if you called them for assistance individually.

## References: Call Early and Call Often

One of the biggest mistakes you can make while job hunting is not to call your references early on in the process. If you wait until the second interview to line up your references, you've wasted a very valuable resource. These are people who think highly of you, your work, and your abilities. If they did not, you would not be asking them to act as references. They also tend to be people who are in senior positions — former bosses, professors, etc. After all, we generally select those who add some lustre. Don't waste these resources, call them now!

Share openly with them your ideas about a career change. Tell them you want to use them as a reference and ask their permission to do so. Then ask them if they know anyone you can talk to as you explore one or more of the new fields. What this does is make your references a part of your job-searching team. They are frequently your most enthusiastic supporters, and are often willing to help you as much as possible.

In 1996, I left the practice of law for a second time, and focussed on a move into consulting. I was eyeing two big firms: William M. Mercer and Towers Perrin. I was at the second interview stage with Mercer. Efforts to attract Towers Perrin's interest hadn't amounted to much, and I was disappointed because I had wanted to explore that option before making a final decision.

To "seal the deal" with Mercer, I was going to need some references. I didn't want to use people at the law firm where I was currently working, or any current clients, because I was afraid it would force my hand. I decided instead to use a former client — a very senior corporate financier for whom I'd quarterbacked a merger transaction two years earlier. I explained what I was up to and asked if I could use him as a reference. The discussion went something like this:

"Sure I'll act as a reference for you. Mercer's a great firm. But before you make a final decision about joining them, shouldn't you also talk to some other firms in that field, like Towers Perrin?"

"Well, I can't seem to get Towers' attention. Meanwhile, things are going well with Mercer. I like them. And I really want to get this put together because we're discussing a start date of Labour Day and it's already August."

"I wish you'd called me sooner because one of my best friends is the head of Towers Perrin. But as it happens I'm playing golf with him tomorrow! Would you mind if I had a word with him and suggest that he call you?"

"No. I wouldn't mind at all."

Less than forty-eight hours later, my phone rang. It was the head of Towers Perrin. "Listen, I was playing golf with Bill yesterday and he suggested I give you a call . . ."

When I think of all the efforts I had made to get this firm's attention, and here was the top guy, just one phone call away. And now he was calling *me*!

Can I promise similar results from all potential references? Obviously not. But I can assure you that references will generally form the most valuable resource in the career-change/job-search process. Make sure you keep references in the loop as the job search progresses. They can often provide new ideas and contacts on an ongoing basis. For example, if you call one of your references saying, "I've been hitting a brick wall on the idea we discussed months back so I'm pursuing something different. I've been reading a lot about Millennium Industries," don't be surprised if he or she suddenly offers a contact at Millennium. Here was a job target you never discussed the first time around.

Of course, the call-early-and-call-often rule *only* applies to references who are not working for your current employer. Your boss must continue to be the last to know about your intentions to leave the fold. Similar caution also applies to former bosses who still work at the company you are planning to leave. If company loyalty prevails over personal friendship, your intentions may not remain a secret very long. This is something only you can gauge.

The most valuable of all references is generally a former boss who has left the organization. Here, typically, is a worry-free reference and ongoing source of support. Those who have left a company are often keen to help others make the break. With the high rate of turnover in most companies today, you may well find someone like this in your not-too-distant past. The next-best alternative is a former boss from another organization where you worked prior to your current employer.

Consider not only those above you in the workplace hierarchy, but those below — people who worked for you and who can attest to your being a wonderful boss. As workplaces become increasingly democratic (or at least fancy themselves to be so!), such references begin to carry increased interest and weight. Just being able to offer them may strike a prospective employer as a "progressive" suggestion. Again, these should *not* be those who report to you in your current position or organization. They should come from the past and include those with whom you built a strong working relationship. These are often the same people who will look to you for a reference next time they change jobs, so there is a quid pro quo.

If your work brings you into contact with clients, customers, or suppliers outside your immediate workplace, consider these as potential references. Many employers value client/customer references, particularly if the move you are planning involves similar client/customer contact. These people are generally excellent networking resources, as they often have many contacts in other organizations that they are happy to provide you with if you call them to request a reference.

Academic references are common, but less relevant if you've been out of school for a while. Consider academic references from night school courses or other more recent experience. Consider also references you know through volunteer work or community work. If you sit on a committee of the city art gallery, a fellow committee member who has witnessed your contribution over the past few years may be a worthwhile choice — particularly if he or she has a credible position (CEO of a well-known company) or if your work with the committee would showcase some of the transferable skills you are looking to apply in the new position.

Another key piece of advice: *Call more potential references than you will ever actually need.* After all, when you finally need them, chances are one or two may be out of town. The real reason, however, is to add more potential references to your search team, and the contacts they provide. If you know twelve people who could all be possible references and none of them is at your current workplace, give them *all* a call, even if you think you'll need only four in the end. Besides, it's nice to have the flexibility to use different people for different kinds of career goals.

It's also impressive to be able to offer an interviewer a choice of references from different aspects of your career, and let him or her choose who to call: "If you'd like some academic references, I'd suggest either my economics professor or the dean of my college but if you'd like to focus on my employment history, I'd suggest my former boss at ABC, who was the controller, or the vice-president of the Widget Division, whom I assisted directly on a number of projects." It looks much more polished than someone scrambling around just before the offer is about to be made trying to track down old Professor Jones who left for Fiji six months ago.

References are worth their weight in gold, and should be treated like gold long after the career change or job search has reached its happy ending. Make sure you call each one of them back once you've found your new job — even if you never used them as a reference. Mention that you used a number of references and felt sure not everyone would be called. For those who did provide a reference, finding out what questions were asked may give you some early insight into your new employer.

For all, a thank-you note is in order and for particular assistance, lunch and/or a small gift would not be at all out of place. Make sure these people are on your Christmas card list. If they are in town, try to call them every six months or so for lunch. They will be interested in your progress in your new career and will feel good about helping you make the move. And if things haven't worked out in the new job, well then, your lunch may serve another purpose . . .

## *Let Your Fingers Do the Walking*

In an earlier chapter, we discussed business directories. In addition to these there are a host of other directories, tailored to many different areas of research. For example, suppose you want to contact someone in the XYZ Corporation and would especially like to talk with someone in the engineering department. You have canvassed your friends, acquaintances, and references in a "six degrees of separation" search but no leads have emerged. Here are some suggestions for directories that may just help you find the elusive XYZ engineer.

## Alumni Directories

If you went to college or university, you may have access to alumni organizations with member lists. These organizations generally publish the names of alumni and their present positions, often with telephone numbers. Perhaps someone from your alma mater is now at XYZ. If you don't have a copy of this kind of directory, call your alumni office and make enquiries. It may cost you a modest fee to join the alumni club or you may have to make a small donation to a fundraising campaign but the directory may yield you some gold!

The best thing about using alumni directories is that the school connection provides you with an instant source of rapport. Don't neglect more recent alumni who may hold more junior positions in your targeted organization. While they probably lack the clout of someone senior to yourself, they can nonetheless be an invaluable resource and may provide you with an excellent set of contacts and insights.

Ask your friends and acquaintances about their alumni directories. If you find someone in a Stanford Business School alumni directory who works at one of your target companies and you went to the University of Toronto, it still may be a useful discovery. From there, you and a friend who attended Stanford can brainstorm about other contacts or classmates who could put you in touch with this person. You might even ask your friend to agree to take you to the next Stanford alumni lunch. Once you know the person's name and approximate age it may be less difficult than you think to pick them out in a crowd.

## Professional Directories

Professional organizations also frequently publish directories of members. So if you're trying to make a contact at XYZ Engineering, the Professional Engineers' Association, or whatever the local engineering association is called, may have a directory. Law, advertising, human resources, finance, dentistry, all have their professional associations. If you are a member of one, you're probably entitled to a copy of the directory, often for free or a modest fee.

If you're not a member, call the professional association and ask if they have a reference copy at their offices available for the general public. You could suggest that you are considering employing someone in this profession and want to use the directory to find some contacts. Since most professional associations view their role as a form of marketing their members, such a request is likely to meet with a warm response.

Make sure you look to friends, acquaintances, and your local library in search of these directories. Some of the most useful ones are not exactly household names. For example, I was unaware that a directory existed of human resource practitioners called the *Human Resource Management Association (HRMA) Directory* until an acquaintance in this field alerted me when I contacted her about doing research into a possible career change.

## Volunteer or Community Directories

Volunteer or community organizations also may provide useful directories. Lists of active members are sometimes published, including their positions and direct phone numbers. For example, Brian J. joined the Ireland-Canada Chamber of Commerce shortly after arriving in Vancouver. Two years later, when he was no longer even a member, he used its directory to make contact with the chairman of a prominent Vancouver organization who happened to be a member. Their mutual Irish heritage and affiliation with the Irish Chamber of Commerce provided common ground that allowed for some rapport to be built right away.

Not all volunteer or community organizations publish membership lists and when they do, they are sometimes very careful to restrict their circulation to members, making them more difficult to find and access if you are not a member. However, most organizations publish information about their boards of directors or club executives. Here, for example, you may find that the vice-president of research at XYZ is on the board of the United Way. If you've been a United Way canvasser, and know people within that organization, you can begin by asking your United Way friends if they've ever met this person and could introduce you. Alternatively, you may want to find out about the next United Way event and be on the lookout for him or her at it. If these two approaches come up dry, you can still call the vice-president and refer to your mutual involvement in the United Way.

## *Turning Events into Opportunities*

One of the biggest mistakes that career changers and job hunters make is to bury themselves in their research and avoid making new contacts. Weekends are a good time for research. During the week, however, make sure you take time to get out and meet some new people who might be helpful to you in your quest.

Look for events that might lead you to new contacts. The closer these events are to your job targets, the better. Even attending functions that have little or no connection to your job targets may provide a few new acquaintances who may, eventually, lead to contacts. The point is to avoid becoming invisible. No matter how unhappy you are in your current situation, or how battered your self-confidence right at the moment, you need to get out there and meet people. Consider the following events as fertile meeting grounds.

— *Seminars, workshops, and courses in a field relating to your job targets.* Attending these sessions provides an opportunity to meet both the lecturers and participants as well as an update on developments in your chosen field. Make sure you arrive early to meet other participants. Ask the lecturers questions, particularly if you think you might like to call them later on. If there is a coffee break, don't stay at your desk reading. Get up and meet as many people as possible in that limited time.

— *Events held by professional associations.* If your primary job target is to be an environmental lawyer and you're currently practising real estate law, find out if the Bar Association has an environmental law subsection and attend their next luncheon or dinner. Finding out about these events may be the biggest challenge. Begin with the professional association. Ask them to fax or mail you (preferably to your home) a list of upcoming meetings. Alternatively, ask your contacts in this field to let you know when an upcoming event is scheduled. Attending an event with a friend in the field increases your chances of making new contacts; he or she will likely introduce you to other people.

— *Events held by business and trade associations.* While these are less focussed networking opportunities, they may still yield some valuable contacts. If you feel comfortable, you might even mention to someone you're sitting beside at lunch, "Does your company do business with XYZ Corporation? I've been dying to meet some of the people there." Your luncheon partner may simply reply, "No. We don't deal with them." On the other hand, he or she might offer, "We don't do business with XYZ but my neighbour is the vice-president of engineering there."

— *Events sponsored by one of your targeted organizations.* If you hear that the president of a company you are particularly interested in is speaking at an upcoming luncheon or that an award for excellence in entrepreneurship is being sponsored by that company, there are likely to be a number of people from the organization in attendance. You can "crash" a company seminar or event, though this is more extreme.

There are, of course, pros and cons to this approach. For instance, don't crash a seminar sponsored by a small organization, where "intruders" can be easily spotted. On the other hand, if Microsoft's worldwide convention is going on at your local Hilton, and Microsoft is your first target company, you might wander into the Hilton lobby that week and see if you can unobtrusively settle into a seat at the back of one of the larger sessions.

— *Events sponsored by clubs, alumni associations, and volunteer organizations.* As discussed above, these events are particularly useful if you have scoured the directories of these organizations and found the names of people you want to meet. Even if these potential contacts aren't there, it's good to get out and meet new people during a search. Some may provide information that could change your direction or pave the way to the very introduction you were seeking.

— *Making the most of business travel opportunities.* If your work involves a lot of travel and you are looking to jump ship, don't forget that fellow business travellers are a good networking resource. Long flights often involve lengthy conversations. If you hit it off with your seatmate why not mention what it is you're thinking of doing? You may be surprised to find that this new friend has some excellent contacts that he or she would be happy to pass on to you.

You might set yourself a goal of attending one of these events every one to two weeks. As you choose events, aim for those held after work, at breakfast, or at lunch. If you are changing careers within your existing field, however, take the opportunity to attend seminars during working hours that are related to your current job. If you're not currently employed in a full-time job you have the opportunity to attend even more of these events.

When it comes to event networking, be sure to keep an eye on your personal budget. Some of these events are expensive, often in the range of $500–$1000 for seminars of a day or longer. While one or two of these may be worth the investment, you won't be able to afford events of this nature on a weekly or even monthly basis, particularly if you have no regular source of income. It may be a good idea to establish a monthly budget for these types of events at the outset. You can then decide if the money is better spent at regular board of trade lunches, or saving up for an international conference in your target field.

When you attend one of these events and meet someone at a company that you are interested in, remember that this introductory meeting is exactly that: an introduction. It is *not* the venue for you to make a pitch about why XYZ Corporation should hire you, nor to pitch any variation on that theme. Resist even suggesting that you are considering a career change into this area. There will be time enough for that later on.

Your conversation should revolve around questions about the organization and the field in general. Make sure that you demonstrate knowledge and interest, but take the role of listener in this introductory conversation. It's the best way to build rapport and find out all you can about the company and the industry. At the end of the discussion, ask your new contact if he or she has a card and suggest that you would like to invite him or her to lunch or coffee sometime.

If the new contact asks why you have so many pointed questions, respond by saying you have a tremendous interest in this field and are doing some research to find out more about it. If pushed, you might offer that you have considered exploring possibilities in this field, but are still in a very early stage in your research and have made no decisions yet. If the new contact responds by suggesting that they are looking for people and you should give them a call, you may see your research phase progress at the speed of light! However, it should be the contact, not you, who accelerates the process to this level in the initial meeting.

## A Case Study in Conference Networking

Steve T. was staffing a booth for his company at a recent conference. Mike, a job hunter hoping to use the conference to make contacts, came over to Steve's booth and asked if the company's national practice leader was available. Suspicious, Steve immediately took to the role of gatekeeper and asked Mike why he wanted to talk to the practice leader. Mike told Steve that he was looking for a job and gave Steve a pitch as to why the company should hire him. He even offered a copy of his résumé. Steve remarked, "He never even asked me what it was that I did, nor did he seem particularly knowledgeable about our firm. Frankly, he seemed desperate to land a new job. While I felt somewhat sorry for him, his approach turned me off and, I have to admit, I wasn't very helpful."

What did Mike do wrong? First of all, he spent little time establishing a rapport with Steve, or showing interest in the organization. "A three-minute conversation, in which he demonstrated some knowledge of our firm, would have made a world of difference," Steve noted. "But he didn't seem to care what it was that we did or what new developments made us interesting as an employer. My impression was that if we could provide him with a paycheque, he would be happy."

Steve also didn't appreciate the "take-me-to-your-leader" approach. Add to that Mike's hurried pitch about why he'd be a good hire, and his quick stuffing of a résumé into Steve's hand, and you have a formula for disaster.

"I really didn't get it," Steve relates. "He spent no time at all trying to build a rapport with me, yet he put me in the powerful position of deciding whether to let him meet the practice leader."

Could Mike have done better? Steve offers some pointers of his own: "We had a number of brochures at our table outlining new services we had recently launched. Some of us were scheduled to speak on them during the convention. He could have come over to our booth, picked up our brochures, perused them for fifteen minutes, and returned, armed with some company knowledge. A more effective opening might have gone something like this: 'I see your firm has moved into performance management lately. Is that one of your specialties personally, or do you focus in another area?'

"Regardless of how that was answered, he could have read the convention agenda and followed with: 'I see that Alice G. of your firm is giving a talk on performance management. Is Alice your practice leader?' This would have got me talking about Alice, or I would have named the practice leader. After this conversation, he might have said: 'You know, I've been doing a considerable amount of work in performance management myself and I'd be really interested in speaking to people at your firm who specialize in the area. Are any of them here? Your practice leader, for example?' Chances are that I would have been much more inclined to provide an introduction."

And what if Steve gave Mike the introduction? Mike would have been equally remiss if he immediately switched gears and started his pitch. A conversation with Alice on the issue of performance management would have been the order of the day, allowing Mike to showcase his interest and experience in this area without ever putting Alice on the defensive by asking her for a job outright.

Preferably, they would have exchanged business cards and have gotten together over lunch or coffee in a week's time.

If, as is often the case at conventions, they didn't live in the same city, two choices emerge. Mike could simply have exchanged cards and called Alice a week or two later by phone, raising the issue of possible employment. If Alice had been sufficiently interested, she might have been willing to fly him in for an interview. Or Mike could have approached Alice before she left, saying, "I really enjoyed our conversation yesterday and I was wondering if you might have a few minutes when we could grab a coffee and continue our discussion."

If the convention was winding up, and there was no time to meet, Mike would need to decide whether to move into the pitch immediately. This would have depended on how strong the rapport was between him and Alice. If they were chatting like old school chums, a pitch might have been well received. If, on the other hand, Mike's relationship with Alice was friendly, but not particularly warm, his waiting to make a follow-up call in a week's time would have made more sense.

## How Event Networking Led Me Through My Latest Career Change

Hypothetical discussions often bring out the skeptic in all of us, so I'll end this section by indulging in a personal story to illustrate how event networking successfully brought me through my latest career change. I had developed an interest in the area of executive compensation consulting and wanted to learn more about it. I particularly wanted to meet people at two of the leading firms in town — William M. Mercer and Towers Perrin.

One friend of mine offered me some contact names out of the *Human Resource Management Association Directory*. But as she personally knew no one at Mercer and a discussion with some of her friends in the industry also came up empty, I held off. Leafing through an alumni directory of my old university business school, I found what I was looking for — a fellow alumni who was not only a Mercer consultant, but whose area of specialization was in compensation. She had graduated several years behind me but was clearly at a level where she could either make a hiring decision or put me in touch with someone who could.

I phoned the alumni association, and while I hadn't attended any of their events in years they were happy to inform me that a luncheon was coming up in two weeks' time. I reserved a ticket. Arriving at the hotel ballroom plenty of time before everyone was seated, I knew I was looking for a young woman in her late twenties or early thirties. I made sure to smile warmly and strike up a conversation with every young woman there. It only took three such attempts before I found her, and I made sure the conversation continued until it was time to be seated for lunch. I sat next to her and found that we got along well.

At no time did I suggest to her that I was looking to change careers into her field. I told her that I found her field fascinating and had been doing some reading about it recently. I asked her numerous questions about recent developments in compensation and about how she enjoyed working at Mercer. She expressed interest in some of the articles I had read recently and I couriered them to her the next day. (Another benefit from time logged in library research!)

A day or two later she phoned to thank me and invited me to lunch. She asked if I'd ever considered a career change into this field. As it happened, they had been looking for a new executive compensation consultant for some time and had actually retained the services of a headhunter to help in the search. In our luncheon, and subsequent interviews with her boss and the national practice leader, I managed to convey my genuine interest in the field and to convince them that my background lent itself very well to this area despite the fact that I had no direct experience. I joined William Mercer less than three months after that alumni lunch. And I made a donation to my alumni association out of my first paycheque.

## *Becoming an Expert in Your New Field*

The quickest way to make connections with experts in your targeted new field is to become one yourself. At the very least, you can involve yourself in a project that puts you into contact with those experts. One of the best ways of achieving this is to write an article relating to one of your job targets. While this may sound presumptuous, your passion, interest, and research in the area may make it quite feasible.

The article might consist, for example, of compiling different views of trends in the field. In order to write this article, you will need to gain the perspective of experts through personal interviews. To add credibility, you might approach a journal, magazine, or newspaper at the outset. Ask if they are interested in publishing this type of article. When you approach people for interviews you can say, with conviction, that you have discussed publication of the article with Journal X or Y.

With the article as your context, it will be easier to call virtually anyone you wish to speak with and set up a meeting. And after that first meeting, you can call them back some time later (an appropriate grace period of several weeks is recommended) to discuss your own interest in making a transition into the field. This turns a "cold call" into a "warm call," making a meeting over coffee to discuss your interest even more likely. And since you have already demonstrated your interest and knowledge of the field, the prospect will have no doubt that you are serious about the transition. Once the article is published, it yields other opportunities. You can refer to it in meetings with other prospects, as it is a tangible demonstration of your sincere interest in and knowledge about the field.

Some job targets lend themselves to writing articles better than others. For example, if experts in the field regularly contribute to journals and articles about new trends, it might be a promising tactic to explore. If, on the other hand, you are targeting an area such as grocery wholesaling, where journal articles aren't the norm, this project may actually mark you as an outsider.

Writing an article may be a more attractive option for people who are jumping ship while still employed. Conducting interviews, writing the article, and getting it published take time. It may be a luxury those who have an existing paycheque can more readily afford. It's also a good strategy if your job target is somewhat related to your current line of work. If you were to tell your current employer that you were writing an article about this field and he or she would scarcely raise an eyebrow, this strategy could be for you!

Under the guise of the article you have the freedom to call and meet with whomever you wish in this field — and can often place these calls during company time! If you are late returning from a meeting with someone you are interviewing for the article, it's probably okay. Don't drag the process on, however, or your employer will lose patience and possibly become suspicious. If, however, you act reasonably and take proper advantage of this situation, it may be very useful in helping you with your career transition. You may even decide to move on to organizing a seminar or giving a speech in this field.

# *Turning Cold Calls into Warm Calls*

By now, your networking notebook pages should be filling up with the names of people you can contact to get more information about the career you are interested in and job prospects in this field. Most people find that the worst part of job hunting is contacting the people you identified in your research and getting them to talk to you. Like anyone receiving a call from a stranger, the recipient is generally cautious, guarded, and often dismissive. To avoid this, you need to turn these cold calls into warm calls.

What exactly is a "warm call"? It can take any of the following forms:

- a call to someone you know or with whom you have previously established a business relationship;
- a call that allows you to refer to a mutual friend or acquaintance;
- a call to someone with whom you have something in common (the same university, church, volunteer organization, etc.);
- a call to someone you have already met and spoken to briefly.

There are varying degrees of warmth. Calling someone you already know is the warmest choice of all. A mutual friend or acquaintance also provides a warm point of entry — there is a sense that you have been pre-screened through your acquaintance with this person. A mutual point of connection, such as the same university, provides a weaker but still valid means of opening the discussion. People are generally more willing to help a fellow alumni or club member than they are a total stranger. Finally, if you have met the person, even briefly, and they vaguely remember you (or at least don't remember anything off-putting about you!) you're still ahead of being a total stranger. *All* of these options are preferable to a cold call.

Remember, too, that warm calls become even warmer when someone calls the contact on your behalf. If the contact is an important one, and your mutual friend or acquaintance would seem willing, you might see if you can suggest the following: "It seems like you know Fred pretty well. I don't suppose you'd be talking to him any time soon and could mention that I'll be calling him? That way he'll know who I am when I call."

This is a fairly innocuous request. The worst your mutual friend can say is no. However, he or she may respond with "I doubt I'll be seeing Fred soon, but I can give him a call and tell him about our discussion so that he'll be expecting your call." This is what you are hoping for! Having an advance call from a friend or acquaintance implies that you are someone worthwhile. Fred will probably be even more receptive and helpful than he might have otherwise been.

Some people wonder if there is a danger that the mutual friend may editorialize during the advance call, perhaps revealing more information than you might wish. In my view, this risk is worth taking for the potential gains it offers. Chances are they are going to discuss you at some time in the future anyway — it is almost always better for the mutual friend to initiate that discussion.

## Calls to People You Found in Your Library Research

If you took down the names of people you discovered in your library research, don't dismiss the idea of trying to make contact with them. Talking with them may give you some incredible leads! While this will technically be a cold call, you can immediately take some of the chilliness out of it by saying that you have read their work or something that's been written about them. Most people are flattered these kind of comments and receptive to the discussion that follows.

It shouldn't be too difficult to locate people found in your research. Most articles reference the position of the person they quote, or of the author. They often say something like "Ted M. is the practice leader of Forensic Accounting for KPMG in the Western United States." Armed with this information, you can call a local KPMG office that can probably provide you with Ted's number in California, Seattle, or Houston. Alternatively, you might try contacting the magazine or journal editor, indicating that you are conducting some research into this area, enjoyed the article, and had some questions for the author.

As with any of your other calls, characterize the nature of your request for information and contacts as "research." Until you actually have the number of the expert in your possession, make sure that you make no reference to the fact that you might be looking for a job. For example, if you were to mention this to the journal editor, you may find that he or she responds by trying to protect the author from unsolicited job queries and is suddenly unable to locate the number.

When you actually get the person on the phone, however, you may want to go a bit further and let them know that you are researching their field from the standpoint of making a career transition. Tell them a little bit about why the field interests you and what elements of your background you see as a good fit. Ask for their comments. "Am I right in thinking this would be a good fit or does it seem to you I'm barking up the wrong tree?" If they say, "Yes, your background would add a valuable perspective that most people in this area don't have!" you can assume that others will feel the same way. This should help you in formulating your "pitch" to a prospective employer.

If, instead, the expert points out that there are sizeable skill gaps between your background and what would be required of someone working in this field, ask how you might best fill those gaps to make the transition. Is going back to school really necessary, for example? Have people without formal training in this field moved into it successfully? If so, what sort of background did they have? Could you contact one or two of these people to talk to them about making a transition into this field? How were they able to go up the learning curve successfully? If they provide you with contact information, it will likely prove to be a *real* windfall. Scarcely will a career changer receive better help than from someone who has already made a similar career transition.

Either way, make sure to ask the expert about the following:

- trends in the field,
- which organizations are considered leading edge, and
- which organizations in your geographic area do high quality or innovative work in this field.

Also ask if there is anyone else (preferably someone in your geographic area) with whom you should talk. While this contact information may be a real treasure for you, it will probably not strike the expert as anything particularly significant that he or she is giving away. After all, you have not said you are looking for a job; all you have asked for is information in the context of researching the field. Besides, if they think you have potential and interesting credentials, they know they will be doing their friends and colleagues a favour by putting you in touch with them.

If a name or names are proffered, ask, "When I contact this person, may I say that you suggested that I give him a call?" They will almost always will say "Sure!," which is the gateway to another warm call.

A note of caution here: Be careful not to ruin this kind of warm call by suggesting that you are somehow a close friend of the expert who gave you the contact name. If the contact subsequently calls the expert and finds out that you have had only one phone conversation, your credibility will suffer dramatically.

## Long-Distance Networking

Long-distance networking is a variation on the theme of contacting people uncovered in your library research. It works like this: You discover the names of some excellent contacts in the field through research, targeting only those who live in cities other than yours. You call these people, explain that you are exploring a career change into their field, and ask if they can recommend anyone you can talk with in your local area.

You'll be amazed at how many contacts they may supply. They are often happy to help when there is no risk to themselves. Because you have not expressed interest in asking for a job, and you are clearly interested in another geographic location, their assistance is relatively risk-free.

As always, ask if you may use their name in calling the contacts they provide. If so, you suddenly have a warm call to a prospect right in your own town! As with the expert, make sure you don't imply that your relationship with the person who provided this information is something more than it is.

## *Bypassing Secretaries and Other Gatekeepers*

In the movie *Monty Python and the Holy Grail*, the knights are forced to answer a series of questions from an old troll before being allowed to cross a drawbridge en route to the Grail Castle. Knights who fail to answer correctly are flung to their deaths into the chasm below.

While most secretaries do not resemble old trolls, they can be similarly intimidating gatekeepers, and equally deadly in keeping you away from the person that you need to talk to. After all, most secretaries view part of their job as "protecting" their bosses from unwanted pests.

The conversation begins something like this: "Hi. I'm calling for George Big. Is he in?"

"Mr. Big is in a meeting. May I help you?"

"No. I really need to talk to him."

"May I tell him the nature of your call?" *This* is the turning point; here are some alternatives for making it across the bridge:

— *Avoid the gatekeeper altogether.* Try to obtain a direct line for Mr. Big. Call early in the morning or in the evening — before or after normal working hours when the secretary is unlikely to be at her desk — but when Mr. Big may be working away in solitude.

— *Answer the gatekeeper by referring to your mutual friend or acquaintance.* "Wendy S. from the ABC Corporation suggested I call Mr. Big regarding some research I'm doing." That is generally enough to get past most gatekeepers. As mentioned above, it works particularly well when the name mentioned is that of an expert in the field. I know first-hand because that's how I got to meet my literary agent, whose secretary was adept at keeping unpublished new writers at bay. When I mentioned that one of his clients who had written a bestseller had suggested I call, I was suddenly put right through and warmly received.

— *Answer the gatekeeper by referring to your mutual point of connection.* "Mr. Big is a fellow alumnus of Old Boys University. I thought he might be able to assist me with some research I'm doing." Don't be surprised if that message gets misinterpreted so that you are listed on the message as being with Old Boys University. But that is a minor matter — unless Mr. Big has very bad memories of the place he is very likely to return the call and any misunderstanding can be quickly resolved.

— *Answer the gatekeeper by mentioning that you have met Mr. Big. (Note: You should only say this if it is true!)* This is for circumstances where you attended the same event as Mr. Big, and you might simply have approached him at the end and asked a fairly straightforward question. It's a short meeting, but it's enough. You would open with "I met Mr. Big at the Professional Club last week where he spoke about the connection between the new tax accounting rules and the prophecies of Nostradamus."

— *Answer the gatekeeper by referring to an article Mr. Big has written.* If you call with a question about the article, the gatekeeper will quickly realize that only Mr. Big will be qualified to answer.

— *If you have no real point of connection and are simply cold calling, answer the gatekeeper by saying that you are doing research in the field and want to talk with Mr. Big.* For example: "I'm doing some research in the area of tax accounting and wanted to talk with Mr. Big." Your "research," of course, is whether tax accounting is the new career for you — but you don't need to share this with the gatekeeper!

— *Rather than engage the gatekeeper in discussion, ask to go directly to Mr. Big's voice mail.* The downside of this approach is that it puts the onus on Mr. Big to call you back, which he may not do. The upside is that you get to leave your own message —

not one editorialized by the gatekeeper. If you do this, keep the message brief, such as: "I'm a friend of Wendy S. and she gave me your number and suggested I give you a call." Then leave your number. Mr. Big will have no idea what the call is about, but he is likely to return it as a favour to Wendy.

Regardless of your approach, and despite the fact that gate-keepers are often frustrating, treat all the people in the organization with the same respect and courtesy you would expect if you were in their positions.

A secretary's reaction to a caller can often influence the boss's opinion. For example, Max B. is a senior management consultant, often involved in hiring decisions. A secretary in Max's office gives him her impressions of every prospective candidate to be interviewed as she drops off their résumés. Max has found her impressions fairly consistent with his own and has come to trust her judgement. If someone has treated her disrespectfully along the way, she will ensure that this is brought to Max's attention before he meets with them. That person unknowingly comes to the first meeting with a big strike already against him or her. The best comment a gatekeeper can pass on to the boss is that you "seem to be very nice." This is not always easy when much of the interaction involves the gatekeeper trying to railroad you away from the contact. But it's well worth the effort!

## *"Send Us Your Résumé"*

If the gatekeeper figures out that you are really after a job, he or she may suggest you send in a résumé. This is a standard line that gatekeepers use to put you off the track. Don't get too excited by this invitation. "Send us your résumé" is generally a dismissive rather than a helpful suggestion. When it is made by anyone other than the person you want to talk with, try to resist.

Sending a résumé at this point unmasks you as a job seeker, often long before your research is complete. At worst, the gate-keeper can use it to deny you access to Mr. Big altogether: "I showed your résumé to Mr. Big, but we're just not hiring right now." This means that you never get an opportunity to give Mr. Big a proper pitch. At best, you will get a chance to see Mr. Big but the tone will assume the seriousness of an interview rather than an opportunity to build common ground.

The most effective way to respond is to say, "Well, I'm not actu-ally looking for a job right now; I'm just researching the field." You might follow that up with "I don't think I even have a résumé pre-pared! Is it really necessary?" If the gatekeeper remains persistent, however, it becomes an increasingly difficult decision — mainly because you begin to wonder whether they may be filling a job in their department and might want to give you a shot at it.

My best advice is to shake off invitations of this nature rather than seizing them like manna from heaven. More likely than not, a casual invitation to send in a résumé is leading nowhere but to a brushoff. However, if you get the sense that there is something more to it, or that your access to the decision-maker will be blocked until the résumé is proffered, you may have to reconsider. The choice is clear, however, when they ask you to "send in a résumé for our files." You can almost be assured that the "files" they are speaking of are round and hollow and sit on the floor under people's desks.

## The Human Resources Department: Why You Shouldn't Be Calling Them — Unless You Are Looking for a Job in Human Resources

Gatekeepers and others will frequently try to steer you in the direction of the human resources department if they get the sense that you're looking for a job. The problem is that most of the time this department functions not unlike an internal headhunting group for the company. That is, people in HR generally engage in interviewing candidates and helping them get an offer *only* when the company has a specific position it is seeking to fill. These include, by the way, entry level positions, which is why many people who had the experience of being hired through HR upon graduation don't balk at the suggestion.

But the rules are different when you are making a mid-career lateral transfer. And even more so when a career change is involved or you are proposing a brand new position. These decisions can only be made by people working within your targeted department. They are the ones who typically control budgets, and they are the ones most capable of recognizing where value can be added in more creative ways.

Human resources departments are generally unlikely to explore these kinds of possibilities. I say "generally" because there are exceptions to this rule. There are some extremely progressive vice-presidents of human resources who are willing to entertain ideas for a new position within the organization, especially if it could be shown to add value. The problem is that you have no way of knowing if the HR people in the company you are targeting are exceptional or more traditional. Unless you have strong reasons for believing otherwise, it's safest to treat all HR people as traditional. This means focussing your efforts on people within the area where you ultimately want to work — and steering clear of HR in the meantime. There is, of course, one huge exception. Human resources is *always* the right place to call when you are after a job in the human resources department.

People in human resources are sometimes the nicest people you will meet in an organization. It is often nicer, however, to meet them when you are sent there by someone who has basically made a decision to hire you and has asked them to provide you with details on the company's human resources packages. When this happens, you may find they are occasionally disappointed that you have secured this plum job without playing by the rules.

But jumping ship is not about playing by the rules. It's about finding your way to a fascinating, rewarding new career in spite of the rules many organizations seem to have adopted that thwart their exposure to talented, creative people who can help to reinvigorate them. I assure you that if you are able to capitalize on the exciting position you are striving to secure, *no one* — least of all those in human resources — will remain disappointed for long.

# The
# Pitch

## Selling the Porsche

Selling yourself to a prospective employer — particularly when a career change is involved — is not unlike selling a fine motor car. Like a Porsche.

If you called someone up and said, "Would you like to buy a Porsche I'm selling?" chances are you would be rebuffed. A direct sales approach is generally too aggressive. A Porsche may be a beautiful car. For many it is a sort of fantasy car. But hardly anyone is going to respond favourably to an initial call like that. They will say, "I'm not looking for a new car right now" or "I can't afford a Porsche" or "I don't like those cars." They won't give you an opportunity to explain the merits of the vehicle.

What if, instead, you called someone up and said you were doing a little research into motor cars and would like their opinion. You invited them down to the Porsche showroom for coffee. While you were both there, the Porsche was driven in, its features discussed. Your guest would have the opportunity to kick the tires a bit and ask questions about the car. At no time would you discuss either the price or the fact that the Porsche was for sale, let alone whether the guest had any interest in buying the car.

What are the chances that at the end of the visit, the guest might have gone home thinking about whether he or she might want to find a place in their garage for that beautiful Porsche? Even if they are not entirely convinced, can you think of a more effective sales presentation? The guest will have spent anywhere from fifteen minutes to an hour discussing the Porsche and its features in a low-pressure environment. Not only do they not feel defensive, they might even warm to the car and its merits.

So it is with job hunting. If you call up a company and immediately ask if there are any positions open, or if they are hiring, you will probably meet with resistance and a litany of reasons why the company cannot hire you. To hire someone laterally requires that the employer be convinced of the value this new hire will bring, because the expense was generally unplanned and unbudgeted.

The Porsche theory is particularly applicable to the career-change process. Career changers often have little chance in competing for a job opening posted in a newspaper because there will be so many others with more direct experience. But career changers also know that their passion, interests, and transferable skills bring something to their job targets that adds value. What they need is an opportunity to make this "pitch" to the right person at a prospective employer. They need to invite the prospective employer down to the showroom and let them take a good look at the "Porsche" and discuss its merits. Hopefully, at the end of the day, the prospective employer will leave having been convinced of these merits and be dedicated to trying to "make a place in the garage" for it.

## *Dos and Don'ts for That All-Important First Call*

Selling the Porsche begins with a warm call to a prospect you have identified in your research and networking as someone who works for an organization that fits one of your job targets. Often this person has the ability to hire you. After working so hard to find this person and make contact with him or her; after navigating your way through a chain of three or four people; and after performing some fancy footwork to get past a gatekeeper, you've made it! That person has picked up the phone and said, "Hello?" *Now what?*

Your first task is to ensure you set the right tone for the call and the subsequent meeting to follow. Whatever you do:

- *Don't* say "I'm looking for a job."
- *Don't* ask "Are you hiring?"
- *Don't* ask "Can I send you a résumé?"
- *Don't* ask "Could I come in for an interview?"
- *Don't* ask "Do you want to buy a Porsche?"

Is that being deceitful? Absolutely not! Until you have completed your research — and completion means talking to this key individual and finding out all you can about the company and your job target — you are *still* gathering information. After all, your job target may look good on paper, but until you meet a few people there and get a sense of the organization, you are not making any decisions. Research, as far as I'm concerned, extends down to casting your eyes over the offer letter. If you don't like what you see, you're not going to work for that organization. Everything that transpired up to that moment was research.

So what *do* you say?

- "I'm considering making a career move and want to talk to some people in the new field I'm interested in pursuing."

— "I'm exploring a number of options right now."
— "I think my background may be well suited to this area, but want to talk with some people in the area."

## DO Your Homework

Before making any calls to a prospect, make sure you have taken the time to conduct some research into his or her organization. This will help you feel more confident. Nothing will destroy your credibility more quickly than saying that you are interested in this field, but acting in a way that shows you do not even know the organization's products, nor that they have recently completed an acquisition that made the front page of the *Wall Street Journal*. You don't need to know biographies of all the senior executives or the fact that they began exporting to Asia in 1974. But you do need to know what they do and what they've been up to lately. Having this knowledge will convey to the prospect that your interest in the field is genuine.

## DON'T Alienate the Prospect

This may sound trite but there are two areas where you can often alienate prospects during the initial call. You need to be aware of them so that you can make sure you don't fall into either of these traps.

Doing homework on a prospect's company creates a double-edged sword. While it is critical to research the subject, it is not good to show off what you know unless you can fit it naturally into the conversation. If you try to impress the prospect by reciting all the facts and figures you can muster, you risk turning them off.

Second, it is normal to seek out organizations where you feel you can make a difference and really add value. But don't point out some problem just to show you could help solve it. This can alienate the prospect right off the bat. Few people enjoy getting a call from someone they barely know who provides them with criticism of their organization. Pointing out problems is risky. It should rarely be done in an initial call. If you feel it is absolutely critical to discuss some of these issues, take time before the meeting to carefully consider how best you can do it. Remember that you may be walking on sacred ground. Don't let it to turn to quicksand under your feet!

## *The Script*

The script for the initial call is something you need to work out in advance. Tailor it to your own personal style so that you feel comfortable with it. Avoid using phrases and language that do not come naturally to you; you will sound stilted.

The call should always begin with reference to the mutual friend or common bond you share with the listener. This is what has transformed that cold call into a warm call. From there, discuss the fact that you are doing some research to help you make a decision about a potential career move. If possible, try to make some reference to the prospect's company that lets him or her know you are sincere enough to have done some homework, without listing off facts and figures like an encyclopedia. The last line is almost always the same: "I was wondering if I could buy you a coffee sometime this week or next and just talk with you about some of these things?"

Below is a sample script for that initial call.

"Hi, Fred. This is Mark W. calling. Wendy S. suggested that I give you a call because she thought you might be able to give me some insight into an issue I'm considering at the moment. I have a background in the airline industry where my focus has been on negotiating international landing agreements.

"The reason I'm calling is that I've become increasingly interested in the area of corporate finance. Not just aircraft financing, but mergers, acquisitions, and taking companies public. Before I seriously consider this kind of a career change, I really want to do my homework and find out all I can about the nature of the work, the industry, and whether my background, or aspects of it, may be a good fit in this area.

"I know Highgrove Capital is one of the most prominent firms in this field here in Merryvale, and that you recently took Titan Corporation public on NASDAQ. Wendy thought you'd be a great person for me to talk with in order to get an idea about what's going on in this area and to give me the sort of insight that would help me in making my decision. I was wondering if I could buy you a coffee some time and ask you a few questions about yourself: how you got into the field, where you see it going, whether you enjoy it, and what sort of backgrounds and skills are particularly well suited to this work."

## Can I Buy You a Coffee?

*"Can I buy you a coffee?"* I have used that line nearly a hundred times in doing this sort of research, and I have rarely had anyone turn me down. (I have never actually bought anyone a coffee in any of these sessions either.) "Can I buy you a coffee?" is a non-threatening question. A coffee means a commitment of fifteen to twenty minutes and an investment of less than five dollars. It is less threatening than a lunch, and it's shorter and cheaper. It's also a lot less threatening than something that sounds like an interview ("Could I make an appointment to see you in your office?"). Coffee is extremely benign.

Don't be surprised if, in response to your offer, the contact suggests lunch or meeting at the office instead. If they do — don't argue! You have held out a non-threatening offer to them and if they are willing to respond with a larger investment, who are you to argue?

If they do take you up on coffee (or lunch or a beer after work), *you* should be the one who offers to pay. You have offered to facilitate the get-together so it should be on *your* tab. You may find that your guest picks up the tab, but never assume anything, and make sure you come to any such meeting fully prepared to cover its costs.

*Your goal at the end of this call is to have set up a brief meeting*, and this should occur within the next couple of weeks. Do not get sidetracked into trying to pitch yourself to your listener prematurely in the call, although you should be prepared to answer questions should they arise. The pitch should take place over coffee, *not* on the phone. Also guard against letting the conversation go on for so long that your listener declines the meeting at the end with a comment like "I think I've really helped you all I can in this call. I'm not sure we need to get together."

## Isn't the Prospect Going to See Through This?

Quite likely the prospect *is* going to suspect, or actually conclude, that your real agenda may be to secure a job. In fact, the term "Can I buy you a coffee?" is already well used in modern business parlance. Many people understand it as a sort of code phrase that really means "Can I talk with you about whether there might be any prospects with your organization or whether you can put me on to anyone else?"

Regardless, prospects are still far more likely to agree to a meeting with someone who has approached the matter in this way. There are a number of reasons for this:

— Positioning the meeting as a brief, information-gathering/ career-exploration session minimizes the risk and time commitment on both sides. The implication is that the prospect will not be put in the position of having to fend off blatant requests for a job. This also means that you must not break the rules by ambushing the prospect and begging for a job the minute you get them alone at Starbucks.

— Because the meeting is brief, the risk of having to defend against direct job requests has been minimized, so the prospect gets to feel good about providing someone with help and insights about their line of work. People generally like to be helpful. Although they may have no intention of hiring you, they may wonder if they can help steer you in the direction of someone who can hire you, or tell you what preparation might be required for this sort of career.

— Prospects appreciate that someone who has taken the time to warm-call them, who appears knowledgeable about the field, and who seems willing to do some work upfront is someone who deserves a little attention. This is a serious, thoughtful, determined person who appears to have a vision and a plan. This is someone worth talking with.

— Even if the prospect thinks they have nothing to offer, it is often useful for them to take a few minutes to meet a potential candidate. Tomorrow one of their staff may resign, or they may need someone in the Los Angeles or Calgary office. Never forget that it is generally every bit as difficult for an employer to fill a position as it is for you to find the right position for yourself. So time taken to meet a fresh face with genuine interest in this field may end up being time well spent by the prospect.

Be prepared to be questioned about your intentions before the prospect will commit to the meeting. A wary person may come right out and ask you if you are looking for a job. It is tempting to respond by saying "OK, let's cut the games. Yes, that's what I'm after. Do you have any openings and when can I start?"

I would urge you, however, to resist that temptation. Until

you actually meet with the prospect and find out more about Highgrove Capital, you don't know for sure if it is the right place for you. And once you say, "Yes. I'm after a job with your company," you have put your hat squarely in the ring without the benefit of additional research. You may find out later that it is not the place for you at all, and then you'll have to back-pedal. Even if the prospect informs you that there would be no point in meeting because there are no jobs at Highgrove Capital, you still want to have coffee with him or her. Make it clear that your primary purpose is gathering information and the fact that there are no jobs at Highgrove doesn't preclude the meeting from going ahead.

Wait a minute! If there are clearly no jobs at Highgrove Capital, why would you waste your time having coffee? Quite simply because the prospect is a person who works in your targeted industry. This prospect will prove to be a tremendous source of insight and possibly a route to other contacts. The outcome of the meeting may be pure research — but it may be valuable research. And there is still an outside chance that your contact may yet "make room in the garage" if they like what they see.

If your prospect asks if you are looking for a job, try to answer "Not at this point. Right now, I'm deciding whether or not this might be a field I'd like to pursue. And if I decide to pursue it, then I'll have to consider in what capacity, and what kind of company might offer the best opportunities for someone with my background and interests. That's where I'm really looking for some insight from you." It is pretty difficult for all but the most hard-hearted of prospects to resist a request for a brief meeting over coffee when it is put in this fashion.

### The Résumé: To Send or Not to Send

Once a meeting is set up with the prospect, it is tempting to want to send a copy of your résumé prior to the meeting, or to bring one along to coffee. But résumés and job hunting go together like a horse and carriage. Once a résumé appears on the horizon, it suggests that, contrary to everything you have just said about doing research, the hunt is on!

Sometimes a prospect will request a copy of the résumé before the meeting. If this happens, there is a tendency to think you have struck gold and that there is a specific job that the prospect is looking to fill. Occasionally, this may be the case. But usually the request simply means that the prospect wants to get a sense of you and your credentials. In most cases such a request will not be forthcoming. This puts the ball in your court in terms of how you deal with the issue of offering the prospect your résumé. Consider one of these two approaches.

### Do Not Send Your Résumé and Do Not Bring Your Résumé to Coffee

This is my recommended approach not only because it is consistent with the idea of a research meeting, but for a number of other reasons as well:

— First impressions are lasting. If you send the prospect a résumé before you meet with them, you put yourself in the position of having your résumé create the first impression. This is a concern if you are attempting a significant career transition. If your résumé illustrates direct experience in the field, as well as some transferable skills, the concern is minimal. But résumés don't easily convey passion and vision. The prospect may decide you don't have the "right stuff" even before you have a chance to make your pitch. Even if you manage to convince the prospect otherwise in the course of your pitch, you have started from a less-than-level playing field.

— By not offering or bringing a résumé, you can determine more clearly what the prospect thinks. If they request a résumé from you *after* you have made your pitch, it may indicate that you've got a bite!

— By not offering or bringing a résumé, you give yourself another opportunity to take one last "kick at the can" if nothing comes out of the meeting. Let's say you have heard nothing further from the prospect and it has now been three or four weeks since your meeting. You felt the meeting went well and you are still interested in the organization. At this point, you may want to phone or write the prospect, saying, "I've done a lot of research and spoken with a number of people in the last month. I'm now convinced that a change from purchasing to marketing is really the right thing for me and I'm ready to pursue a job in this field. I was most impressed with Big Bucks Corporation and some of the interesting strategies your group is pursuing in this area. I'd very much like to send you a résumé so that you might consider whether you'd have any interest in having me join your team."

— If the prospect specifically asks for a résumé, either at the outset or in the course of the meeting, by all means make sure that you send one over by the next day. This means you should have one ready even if you don't intend to bring it to the meeting.

### Bring the Résumé to Coffee

By bringing the résumé along to coffee you give yourself the option of either having it on hand should it be requested or volunteering it without prompting.

— If you want to volunteer your résumé while you sip your lattes, offer it as a reference tool in your conversation. After all, part of what you have asked the prospect's advice on is whether your background might be appropriate. You might say something like "I brought along a résumé — it's not even that up to date — but it should help me remember the things in my background that I feel may allow me to make the transition to this new field."

— Ask the prospect to provide comments on whether this résumé properly highlights the skills and experience that would be most relevant to this new career. This involves the prospect in mulling over the highlights of your background and considering them in relation to the new career you are after. The prospect may end up "selling himself" on your credentials to move into this new field, which is precisely what this meeting was all about in the first place. Even if this doesn't happen, their comments will provide you with some excellent feedback on your résumé and how to position your skills and experience to be most attractive for the job you are seeking. This feedback will come directly from the horse's mouth.

— Make sure you send a revised copy of your résumé to your prospect about three or four weeks after your meeting, modified to include their suggestions. If you do this with a number of prospects, make sure you manage to remember whose suggestions are whose when you send out updated résumés later on.

## Welcome to the Showroom

OK. Résumé in hand (or not), you've arrived at Starbucks, and your prospect is heading towards you. They may not yet realize it, but the two of you have now entered "the showroom." The essence of this little meeting is two-fold:

— You need to find out as much information as you can about this new field as well as potential opportunities with your guest's company and other organizations that might be hiring in this area.

— You need to demonstrate that you have genuine interest in this new area, that you have developed knowledge of it from doing your homework, and that there are aspects of your background that would make you especially valuable in this field.

## Preliminary Questions for Your Guest

It is only polite (not to mention expected) that you will let your guest begin the talking. Most people are delighted to talk about themselves and their careers. It is not only good manners but an excellent way to build rapport and learn as much as you can at the outset. Moreover, your guest typically enters the showroom already wary that you are really a job hunter in disguise. If you open with your pitch, you will confirm this suspicion and the tone of the meeting may be negatively affected as a result.

You will want to develop a series of preliminary questions for the beginning of your discussion. Some examples could be:

— How did you first get interested in this field?
— How long have you worked in it?
— Have you always been with Highgrove Capital?
— If not, where were you before and how was that different from Highgrove?
— What are some of the things you enjoy most about this field? What's fun about it?
— What are some of the most interesting things you've worked on in your career?
— No job is perfect. What are some of the frustrations in this line of work?
— Is there much turnover in this field? If so, why do people leave?
— Would you say the field is growing? If so, what do you believe is leading to that growth and what changes might you foresee happening in this area in the next few years?

— Who would you say are the top companies in this field? What makes them the best?

— Did you ever think of working for any of these other organizations? If so, what made you decide against them?

If at all possible, you should try to work in at least one or two questions that demonstrate to the prospect that you have done a little bit of homework:

— I have read that XYZ Corporation does a lot of exporting to Asia. Have recent developments in that economy affected your business?

— I understand that Highgrove Capital sponsored the underwriting that took Titan Corporation public on NASDAQ last year. Can you tell me more about that transaction and about the kind of work that people at Highgrove would have been involved in to undertake this initial public offering?

— I know that earlier this year your newspaper, *The Daily Press*, acquired *The Daily Times*. Do you still run these two as completely separate newspapers or do some writers and editors have responsibilities for both publications? Do you foresee that both papers will continue to be published as they have in the past?

— Have the cutbacks in government funding affected the courses offered at Whitesands College? I saw recently that you had competed a joint venture to consolidate some of your courses with those offered via teleconferencing at Forest Polytechnical. How is that one working out? Do you foresee more of these sorts of arrangements?

Unless you find yourself sitting across from someone who is either monosyllabic or dysfunctionally introverted, even three or four of these questions ought to be good for a solid ten to fifteen minutes of conversation. In the process, you will learn a great deal. You will gain excellent insights into this field, and catch a glimpse of whether this is the sort of place for you. You will also discover the names of other employers that you need to put in your networking notebook.

## Don't Just Ask the Questions: Make Sure You Listen to the Answers

There is a tendency to view this part of the meeting as the warm-up to your own pitch, and to politely go through the motions rather than really listen to what your guest is telling you. As difficult as it sometimes is to concentrate when your mind is racing ahead to your part of the show, try not to get distracted in this way. Listen, watch the way your guest responds to your questions. If you see there are some big problems in this field, or with this prospective employer — *listen up!* — it is foolhardy to ignore these important signals. You may save yourself from a potentially disastrous choice.

## Now It's Your Turn

Once you have gained some valuable insights, and built up a rapport with your guest so that you are both beginning to feel a little more at ease, it's time for you to make your pitch, which is something you need to have worked out carefully in advance. A different pitch needs to be crafted for each of the three job targets. Practise your pitch a few times before you meet with your guest. A reference or friend may make a good audience.

Although prepared in advance, the pitch still needs to fit with the tenor of the conversation. For example, if you were really keen on a particular aspect of the job, such as going to court for a prospective trial lawyer, and your guest has just finished telling you that you will spend more time on paperwork and motions than in the courtroom, you may need to tailor your pitch.

## A Great Pitch

A great pitch draws on the three major areas you outlined while setting your job targets. It forms the following equation: *Passion* + *Vision* + *Background* = *A Great Pitch*.

— *Passion:* While there is no need to wax dramatic, the truth is that most people would rather hire and work with people who have fire in their eyes for their line of work than those who have that deer-in-the-headlights look. If you are discussing one of your three job targets, this should be a topic that you have more than a passing interest in. Your genuine enthusiasm for the field is something you need to convey to your guest. How far you go is something you can gauge by your guest's response to your questions. If he or she is clearly a little soured on the area, modest enthusiasm is the order of the day. If the responses suggest this is someone living and breathing their work with undeniable pleasure — let them see that there's passion on your side, too. In the latter case, chances are you may just have made a valuable friend and/or a potential boss or coworker!

— *Vision:* If you have done your homework, you should have some ideas about the direction this field may take in the future. Let your guest see your vision. This is something that tends to set apart those who view themselves as having a job from those who view themselves as having a career. A career involves the long term. Having vision also indicates that you are someone who will lead the organization in capitalizing on new trends and remaining in the forefront — an important asset in a competitive marketplace.

Who would you rather hire? Someone who tells you, "I wanted to talk to you about becoming a trial lawyer because I did well at debating in law school and I am tired of doing corporate law" or someone who says, "I'd be interested in your perspective, but I think the increased use of arbitrators as an alternative to going to court has interesting ramifications for trial lawyers. Personally, I would be interested in learning not only how to work with arbitrators, but possibly in becoming an arbitrator myself. I think that being able to offer clients a perspective from both sides of the bench may be really valuable. And if the arbitration trend takes off, there will be no lack of work in this field. What do you think?"

To be most effective, vision should be demonstrated *modestly*. You may alienate your prospect if you come across too much as a know-it-all. You may also want to use your preliminary questions to determine whether the vision you are about to offer is something your guest is likely to agree with. Throw in a question or two at the outset to gauge whether they see things in the same way. If that doesn't seem possible, you can couch the vision statement in more ambiguous terms, by asking if they agree or disagree with some of your views. This allows your guest to take issue with your vision and enables you to listen and respond to these comments gracefully.

Expressing vision is a risk. If your guest agrees, he or she will see you as a thoughtful person with a solid understanding of this field — positioning you exactly where you want to be. If your guest disagrees with your vision, however, it may bring you down a notch in their estimation. Consider this disagreement carefully, however, as it may be revealing. If your vision was formed based on solid research and what you believe to be a good understanding of the field, are *you* really wrong or is *your guest* the one who is actually out of touch? And if the latter is the case, do you want to work with him or her?

— *Background:* The most important aspect of the discussion will be to convince your guest that your background would be of considerable benefit in this line of work — even though you may have no direct experience in this area. In preparing for this part of the discussion, you need to focus on the transferable skills you have gained from your education and work experience, and determine which of these have the greatest relevance to the new area you are targeting. Your task is then to showcase these skills and other relevant accomplishments in the course of the discussion.

Be prepared to acknowledge that there are holes in your background, that you may experience a sharp learning curve or may need to take some additional courses. But don't forget that employers are beginning to understand that people who bring a breadth of experience to a position have something to offer which may be different and valuable from those following a more traditional career path. Tell your guest what you have to offer, why you think this would be valuable in the new field and ask whether this background is enough to make the transition. Then ask what you should consider doing to fill the "skill gap" as quickly and effectively as possible.

Showcasing those aspects of your background that provide a clear and relevant benefit may be more powerful than you think. Most employers know that it is easier to teach someone about an industry than it is to give someone creative problem-solving skills. If you can convince them that there is enough substance in your background to warrant taking the time and the trouble to teach you about the specifics of their field or industry, you may be able to jump ship. When such a background is combined with passion and vision, your odds of jumping ship increase dramatically.

*The Script*

The pitch itself follows a very simple format and generally looks something like this:

— Here's what it is that I'm doing now;
— Here's why I'm thinking about moving into this new field;
— Here's why this new line of work turns me on;
— Here's what I have in my background that I believe would make me especially well suited to this new line of work.

It is generally then followed with a series of statements that sound something like this:

— "Career change is a big decision."
— "I want to talk with a lot of people before deciding what I want to do."
— "I'm looking to gain some insight into this field."
— "I really appreciate your insight and advice."

These are deliberately worded to create a non-threatening environment for the guest. At no point do you ask for a job or whether there are any openings at his or her company. Allow the guest to leave the meeting feeling good about having helped you. Do not force him or her to say "no" to you.

No one, however, is fooled about what has really gone on in that session. You have presented your most convincing arguments for exactly why you might be the sort of person Highgrove Capital should consider bringing on board. You have done so on your own terms — slowly allowing the person to warm to you, demonstrating your skills, passion, and vision.

You have accomplished much more in this little meeting than most people ever have the opportunity to accomplish in an interview. Unless your guest is completely naïve (and therefore someone you would hardly want to work for or with!), he or she will mull over the prospect of finding a place for you at Highgrove Capital several times during the meeting — and may continue thinking about this for days and even weeks to come. You have not tried to sell your guest on hiring you — you have presented them with every possible argument to sell *themselves* on that very idea.

Obviously, the great unknown is whether hiring is even a remote possibility at Highgrove Capital. Perhaps Highgrove is facing difficult financial circumstances and can't afford to take anyone on. Or perhaps they have recently hired. Was your meeting a waste of time? Hardly! If you have favourably impressed your guest, they may be willing to put you on to another prospect where opportunities *do* exist. To facilitate this, always make sure that you have asked these questions at some point before your meeting ends.

— "Who else do you suggest that I talk with in this field?"
— "Do you know the name of someone at those other companies you mentioned who would be good to talk with?"
— "Can I tell them that you suggested I give them a call?"

## The Dress Rehearsal

If you have never networked your way into a job, or had a meeting with anyone over coffee to deliver this sort of a pitch, and you are feeling a little nervous, you are not alone. Why not consider a dress rehearsal?

### Dress Rehearsal in Another City

If your current job involves some travel, you may consider doing a dress rehearsal by going after your job target with an employer in another city. Cast around in the usual way for some contacts in the city you will be visiting. If it's New York, for instance, see if you have any friends or acquaintances who can put you in touch with prospects there. Or maybe your library research will provide you with some names. Place the usual calls indicating that you are considering a career change and are doing some homework. Indicate when it is that you are planning your next trip to the Apple and see if you can line up a few "coffees" while you're there.

While you may debate the value of spending time on this sort of exercise if you have no real intention of moving to New York, there are a number of reasons to consider it. First and foremost, it is an opportunity to test out the process in a risk-free environment. From this experience, you may pick up some important insights that will help you when it comes time to do it "for real" back home. If your approach is well received, it will give you confidence; if not, you will be able to make necessary changes before you approach a prospect that matters.

If things went well in New York you may be able to use the contacts you have made there to put you in touch with some good contacts in your home town. If a New York prospect comes back to you with an offer, you can always reply by saying "I am getting more and more interested in the field, but I have since discussed moving to New York with my spouse and unfortunately that is just not an option for us at this time. I don't suppose you might know anyone in Merryvale that I could explore possibilities with?" You know what they say about New York — if you can make it there, you can make it anywhere! Besides, you may end up changing your mind and looking for apartments on the Upper East Side after all!

### Dress Rehearsal with a Low-Priority Job Target
Rather than run the risk of learning through trial and error on your top job target, consider starting with the least important one. If you make mistakes here, all is not lost — you've still got your most desirable job targets, as well as insights on how to do better

the next time around. Ironically, the biggest problem isn't failing, it's being successful. An offer here may manifest itself before you have even had the opportunity to make some warm calls for your other targets.

If you are dying to leave your job or are presently out of work, a bird in the hand will seem worth a great deal more than a chance at something you would like better. One strategy to keep them at bay is to tell prospects that you are still researching this field as well as some other possible choices, and you have yet to complete the process. While you enjoyed talking with them and have found their organization very interesting, you still feel you need more time to be sure this is the right move. There is no guarantee they will give you more time, but at least you will not be back-pedaling. Your position is entirely consistent with what you said when you first approached them.

If you turn the offer down in this way to explore other job targets, all may not be lost if the other options fail to work out. There is no harm in going back to the employer who made the initial offer sometime later. You can simply say that you have finished your research, found the prospect of working at their organization the most appealing, and wonder if the offer still stands. They might say no if they have already hired someone to fill the position. They might also say yes. And you can accept that offer with fewer regrets, having done your research on the other job targets.

## "Hey! I Don't Have a Lot of Time — I'm Unemployed — or About to Be!"

The jumping-ship approach is clearly most workable for those who still have a regular paycheque and who therefore generally have more time to find a new position. People who lack this luxury sometimes find it tempting to accelerate the process. To some extent, that's fine. In fact, when you tell a prospect that you are "between jobs," they won't necessarily believe that you're just "looking around at all kinds of opportunities." The prospect knows that you are in the market — and available to start work almost immediately. If they want to hire you, they will. Trying to "hard-sell" yourself over coffee instead of sticking to the script is not likely to make a difference, and you risk alienating the prospect by coming across as desperate.

What you need to do in these circumstances is change the tone slightly. That's all. Tell the prospect that you are "between jobs" and while you want to explore a number of opportunities, realistically, your time is limited. If they give you a number of new leads and contacts, ask which one would be most likely to be hiring in the near future. Or come right out and ask if they know of anyone looking to fill a position like this right now.

For those who are not working, it makes sense to use traditional methods of job hunting alongside the jumping-ship process. This keeps every possible iron in the fire. If one of the traditional methods yields you an offer, but the jumping-ship meeting over coffee was for a job that you'd far prefer, you have ammunition to go back to your prospect in a subsequent call. You can tell them that you have an opportunity in your current field, but indicate that your preference would be to move into the area you outlined over coffee. Ask if they have any opportunities you should consider before snapping up this other offer.

Even if you are unable to generate your preferred job target right away and are forced to take another position to meet mortgage payments, you have laid important groundwork. You have made one or more excellent contacts in this new field and you have given them your pitch. Keep in touch with these contacts. Once you start receiving regular paycheques you can bide your time until something materializes in this new field that would make you happier than the job you were forced to take to meet your financial needs.

Also bear in mind that even though the jumping-ship process may seem as if it will take a long time, those who generate at least three to four coffee meetings a week and continue at this pace for at least six weeks typically start to see serious discussions and even offers begin to materialize within the same time frame.

## It Ain't Over Till It's Over

### Thanks for Everything

Protocol demands a thank-you note to your guest — within two to three days of the meeting. Nothing fancy is required, just a simple card with a few handwritten sentences. If a friend or other business contact gave you the lead, a call should be placed to that person within a day or two of the meeting to express your thanks and provide him or her with some of the highlights. This call is not only good manners, it provides you with two opportunities:

- to further engage your friend as a member of your job-hunt support network and see if they have any other ideas for net-working contacts; and
- to see if the prospect has called your friend after the meeting and expressed anything to them about you.

### Don't Turn into Pavlov's Dog

The meeting is over. You sense that it went well. The prospect even requested a copy of your résumé, and you've sent it, along with a thank-you note. There's nothing more to do now than sit back and wait for the phone to ring, right? Wrong! The phone might ring but it also might *not*. Don't allow yourself to turn into Pavlov's dog, waiting to salivate at the ring of the bell.

Remember that you have set three job targets for a reason, namely to avoid putting all your eggs in one basket. Now, more than ever, it is time to get busy! Have a look at that last To Do list in your networking notebook and make some more calls. Get on down to the library and see what new information and leads you can turn up. You may find it useful to concentrate on a different job target at this point, which may give you fresh energy.

Think how much more interesting it would be to receive offers from two, or even three, of your job targets. Then you would be deciding not only between employers but between lines of work! While this could be confusing, it would also be unquestionably delightful.

And if that little meeting over coffee really did go well, there is yet another factor to consider. The downside of getting an offer from the prospect's company is that you suddenly have to make a decision about accepting that offer without having fully explored all of your *other* options! You may have very little time left to explore other opportunities before a decision will be required from you. Make the most of the time you have left! Meet as many more people as you can. Fill up your Starbucks frequent buyer card with cappuccinos purchased for still more prospects!

### Stirring the Pot

Okay, three weeks have gone by. You are out generating new leads and meeting more prospects, but you are *still* interested in that first one. You continue to check your voice mail regularly, hoping to hear the dulcet tones of that first prospect leaving a message like "I've thought a lot about our discussion and if you're serious about making this kind of a move, there are some other people at our firm I'd like to arrange to have you meet." Alas, no such message turns up. This is when you can begin stirring the pot.

First of all, don't forget that the prospect should have given you some names of other contacts in the field. Follow up on those leads. Take them out for coffee. Then call the initial prospect back with a thank-you and an update on those meetings. This accomplishes a number of things: It refreshes their memory of you, it lets them know that you are serious about making a change, and it may make them realize that you are now talking to potential competitors. You would be amazed how many organizations suddenly find openings for people they view as high potential and do not want to see working for their competition. A simple "I wanted to let you know that I gave Jim S. at Transmountain Capital a call and had a very informative meeting with him. I just wanted to thank you again for giving me his number" will do.

Second, after several more weeks you can make one last-ditch attempt to get the prospect to come up with an offer by saying, "I wanted to call you because, as you know, I've been doing a lot of research and meeting a number of people. I've come to a decision that corporate finance is something I really want to pursue. Of all of the people I talked with, and of all the companies I've researched, you would be my first choice. I was wondering if there might be any possibility of our discussing this?"

At this point, you have finally put it squarely on the line. You have shown the prospect that you are a thoughtful and thorough person who has taken time to research a number of opportunities, and you have paid them a compliment by indicating that they are at the top of your list even after all your research. If that isn't the kind of person most employers want to hire, I don't know what is!

Of course, there is no guarantee that even after stirring the pot you'll be given an offer. If not, you should be able to cross that prospect off your list (however reluctantly!), secure in the knowledge that you have done everything possible to convince them to bring you on board. You will have left a good impression, and possibly made more networking contacts on the way to your ultimate new job. The person he put you on to at Transmountain

Capital may be the one to make you your first offer! Or the person at Highgrove may say to a friend at Lakeside Capital some weeks later, "I met this really interesting person over coffee a few weeks ago. We have a hiring freeze right now and there is no way I could even consider bringing this person on board with us — but I was sure impressed! Maybe you'd like to talk with him?"

And so it goes . . . somebody knows somebody who knows somebody who will be convinced by your passion, your vision, and your background that you are someone who deserves a chance at your job target. Although you have worked hard — much harder than someone who has received a call from a headhunter or who has answered an ad in the careers section — you have worked towards your own job targets, which you carefully considered, not some pie-in-the-sky notion that seems better than another day at the current salt mine. Sooner or later your pitch will have its desired effect. A rope, perhaps two or three, will be thrown in your direction. And you will jump ship, while everyone around you will comment on what a great job you found, how happy you are, and how easy you made it all look!

# Surviving Your Career Transition

## It's Easier to Find a Job When You Have a Job

### The Upside: Value, Time, and Tools

There are some significant benefits to trying to find another job while you still have one.

- If you maintain your job while looking for another, you create the perception that you are valued and will have to be "lured away" from your present position. Most people will assume that your current employer is happy with you; it is *you* who are not happy with them, and this has a strong psychological effect that works in your favour.
- A regular paycheque provides comfort. If it ceases and you begin to eat into your savings, you'll feel pressured to find a new source of income. If an offer comes quickly for your lower-priority job target, you may grab the "sure thing" without fully exploring other, more interesting, opportunities.

Maintaining a steady income while you search broadens your focus and changes your priorities. Often, it allows you to pursue passions more easily.

— Your current job may provide you with access to tools that will facilitate your job search. The computer on your desk, the printer down the hall, the laptop computer you can take home, the fax machine, the voice mail. Even little things like staplers and paperclips are there in abundance, ready to be used.

### The Downside: Cloak and Dagger

There is a major downside to trying to find a job while you still have one. In most cases you will have to hide your intentions from your present employer. Often this leads to a whole host of subversive job-hunting strategies.

If you are in a job that regularly requires you to attend meetings outside the office, you are in an excellent position to use this time wisely. You can quite readily get yourself off to meetings over coffee — perhaps two or more a week — without raising a single eyebrow. It's more difficult, however, if you're stuck in the office. There are only so many dentist's and doctor's appointments you can have before creating suspicion. Your coffee meetings will have to be scheduled either before work, over lunch, after hours, or on the weekends. All of these are generally quite acceptable from the standpoint of a prospect who realizes that you are currently employed and respects the fact that you do not want to jeopardize your present employment. You may also come up with some more creative solutions to the problem.

John B. was trying to change careers while still employed at his telecommunications company. After setting job targets and doing some exploratory research, he needed time to meet with prospective contacts. To free up his schedule, John told his boss that he wanted to take a Spanish class at a nearby college. He indicated it would take an hour every day for a month and offered to make up the time by coming in early each morning. When his boss agreed to the arrangement, John had the luxury of an hour every day to meet with prospects, make calls (he used his car phone), or conduct research.

If you have an office with a door, you're in luck because you can shut the door when you wish to make calls to contacts. If the corporate culture at your office is that people never shut their doors, you can devise a strategy to overcome this problem. Some people have complained of migraine headaches or noisy coworkers down the hall. Others have spread word among their colleagues that they are involved in a difficult personal situation at the moment — medical or marriage problems spring to mind. When they then close their office doors to make a call, it attracts little attention.

Maria C. lacked the luxury of an office. Her open workplace afforded little privacy in which to call contacts or prospects. Undaunted, Maria used unoccupied meeting rooms to place such calls for about fifteen minutes each morning and afternoon. Maria favoured meeting rooms on other floors — out of the sight of curious coworkers, who assumed she'd gone for a coffee break. On one occasion, she used the company infirmary to place an important call when all the meeting rooms were in use.

Having access to the facilities at an office can be a tremendous asset in your search, but try to be fair. You should find a way to pay for any incremental expenses that you may incur during your search.

Melissa J. was using her employer's fax machine and printer for her job search. She also made the odd long-distance call after hours. The costs to her employer were minimal, but Melissa wanted to be fair to her employer and pay any incremental expenses herself. She thought she could set up a separate account for these expenses, but she didn't want to raise any eyebrows. In the end, she told the office administrators that she had become the secretary of her local wine-tasting club. Because of this role, she would need to fax information to members. The company set up a separate account, and Melissa's conscience was greatly relieved.

Even if your conscience isn't as bothered as Melissa's, there are very practical reasons to ensure that you (rather than your employer) are covering these sorts of expenses. If you are ever caught by your employer, you will certainly wish that you had. Not only will this be embarrassing — it may be grounds for dismissal.

The cloak-and-dagger approach to finding a job while you are still employed can take its toll. Secrecy can cause stress and anxiety. You can become frustrated by only being able to call a few contacts a week, feeling your current job is taking time away from your job-search efforts. Despite the prevailing wisdom that it is easier to find a job when you have a job, you begin to wonder if you wouldn't actually do much better without one!

## Before You Resign ...

Resigning without having secured another job may become necessary as you shift your job search into high gear. Some people need to pull the plug before they can devote themselves fully to a new search. If this is your preferred approach, make sure that you have laid some solid groundwork first:

— Build up a "job-search fund" out of your regular paycheques and try to put off handing in your resignation letter until the fund is enough to tide you over at least two to three months. Popular wisdom encourages banking a year's salary, though that's often an unrealistic goal for most people to attain. Six months would be great if you can muster it. From the time that you realize that you need a change, try to regularly put away some money for the search. Remember that, if you resign, you will not receive a severance package and your savings will be your primary source of financial support until you find something else.

— Hold off your resignation until you have made considerable progress with your career transition. Developing job targets, conducting library research, and networking should already be well under way. The resignation will then free you up to "conclude the process." If you are well on your way before you leave your present job, this conclusion phase is likely to take less than two or three months. If you haven't done much, you may want to stick it out at your current workplace (however difficult) until you have made sufficient progress. This will minimize the time frame between your resignation and when you actually secure your exciting new job.

## Working Notice

Rather than resigning outright, consider the idea of "working notice." This may be a real alternative if you are considering an out-and-out resignation in order to further your job search. It may also be an answer for those who are caught job searching by their present employer.

Asking for working notice simply means telling your employer that you are not happy and that you intend to begin looking for alternative employment. Rather than resigning before you have found another position, you are asking for a notice period. This means that you will "wind down" your job over the next two months, continue to fulfill your responsibilities, enable the employer to find a replacement, and agree to train that replacement. For your part, you will want to be able to use company time over the notice period to help secure a new position.

Working notice in some ways provides you with the best of all worlds. You can continue to tell prospects and contacts that you are currently employed, and you can use the office facilities without constantly looking over your shoulder. You can actually use coworkers as references and a source of contacts because you have laid bare your true intentions. Best of all, you will continue to receive your regular paycheque throughout the notice period.

This approach also gives your employer a chance to make you an alternative offer. Your boss may not have realized that you were so unhappy, and if they think you are valuable they may come up with something more attractive. This may be something you look at seriously or it may be "too little too late," but having the option can't hurt.

Working notice also benefits the employer by facilitating a smooth transition between you and your replacement. This would not be the case if you simply walked out the door. Working notice does have its downside, however. There is no guarantee that your employer will respond favourably. If you have a boss who makes Cruella de Vil look like Mother Teresa, you can be almost assured that, having tipped your hand about your intentions to leave, you will be told, "Get out now!" If you are not well prepared this can be a devastating reaction.

Before you ask for working notice, consider two key factors: your relationship with your employer; and the length of time you have worked there. The former will give you some insight into how you will likely be treated. The latter will tell you how much severance they will legally be required to give you.

If you discuss working notice with your boss but do not actually resign, and they respond with "Get out now!" you will have effectively been fired. In most jurisdictions, this means they owe you severance. If your tenure with the company is short, the severance will be small, so it doesn't cost them much to fire you on the spot. If, however, you have been there for several years, the severance payment could be hefty. In these circumstances, the employer may prefer to allow you to continue working for a couple of months rather than draft you a big severance cheque. If you are seriously considering asking for working notice, you should consult a lawyer before making the request. For a fairly minimal consulting fee, the lawyer should also be able to tell you what kind of severance you would be entitled to, as well as how best to phrase your request in view of current laws on constructive resignation and dismissal.

If your employer agrees to a working-notice arrangement, they are likely to stipulate a clear time period. Most will agree only to a two- to three-month working notice (and some only to one or two months) because business goes on, and a "lame duck" can only expect to be kept around for so long. If you have some specific skills that will be extremely difficult to replace (especially high-tech knowledge), your employer may be more lenient. Training a new person is foremost in their minds, and they may allow you to stay longer while this training is completed.

You can also suggest adding your unused vacation time to the working-notice period to stretch it out by a week or two. Still, by the time you discuss a working-notice arrangement you should ideally be far enough along in your job search to limit the time you'll need to complete your career transition.

## A Coach and Cheering Section

### Using a Coach

Undergoing a career transition can be demanding, exhausting, and emotionally draining — not unlike running a marathon. Athletes who subject themselves to gruelling endeavours often find it helpful to have a coach. Career changers and job hunters can often benefit from coaching in exactly the same way.

The coach serves largely as a source of ongoing support. They can help you keep going and make sure you don't give up. But remember that it is always up to the athlete to win the game. The coach can serve as your sounding board, but can never make decisions for you. Your coach has no role in developing your job targets. Once you develop those targets, however, you may look to your coach for input and ideas. Your coach can brainstorm with you from time to time; he or she can review draft résumés and help you formulate and rehearse your pitch. First and foremost, however, your coach's role is to contact you regularly and meet with you at least once a week for thirty to forty-five minutes throughout your job search.

If you are undertaking a job search while currently employed, having a coach allows you to avoid the temptation to share the ups and downs of your search with those often closest to you — your coworkers. If you are not currently employed, loneliness can set in and your discipline can wane. Rather than spending an afternoon at the library researching one of your job targets, you may decide to take in a matinee. But your coach can help you keep to your schedule.

There are no hard and fast rules for choosing a coach. Some people like to assign this role to a spouse or "significant other." This involves their partner in the process and lets them share their trials and tribulations with the person they are closest to. Others find this *too* close. They prefer a coach who can be more objective, and who has no personal stake in the outcome of the search.

Other choices could include someone who has already been through a career transition and can offer you the benefit of personal experience; one of your references who has already mentored you during some part of your career; or a good friend who is not a coworker. Having a coach is not for everyone. But if you like the idea and think it could work as a survival strategy through your career transition, you may want to try it.

## Finding a Cheering Section

Whether or not you use a coach in your career transition, there is one integral component of the search that *no one* should be without — a cheering section which acts as a support network. The cheering section takes a more passive role than a coach. It is a special group of friends to whom you can sound off as you endure the ups and downs of the career transition process.

If you are unhappy in your career, you may feel you have to go through the entire transition process alone. You worry that friends and family will react unfavourably to the news that all is not well in your current career. Parents, spouses, friends, and former colleagues may question your sanity: "What do you mean you are unhappy? You are a vice-president making a six-figure salary working for a prestigious company! You should thank heaven for such a wonderful job!" This is exactly what you *don't* need.

What you *do* need is someone to be your cheering section — someone who will appreciate your frustrations and will support you in stepping up to the plate and going after the job of your dreams. You don't need a cheering section big enough to fill SkyDome. You need a few trusted and trustworthy souls who will believe in you and what you are trying to do, and who will regularly lend a sympathetic ear along the way.

Find yourself a cheering section! Years later, with your career transition successfully concluded, and an exciting new phase of your life underway, you will look back on those people who helped to cheer you on through your career change with sincere appreciation. Their encouragement, their understanding, and their friendship will have helped you change your life.

# *After You Jump*

## *Take Advantage of All You Have Learned*

It has taken a lot of effort and time. There have been ups and downs; times when you wanted to give up; times when you cursed the fact that the Job Fairy wouldn't simply land on your shoulder, relieving you of all this work and anxiety; times when it seemed you would never get the break you needed; times when you thought the door of opportunity had finally opened, only to have it slam again quickly; times when you wondered if you shouldn't just have stayed in your previous career, as dissatisfying as it was; or times when you wanted to take something equally unsatisfying, just to make a change! At the end of it all, however, you find yourself pretty much where you wanted to be. You sit back, take a deep breath, and smile, realizing that *you* made it all happen.

Think of everything you did to get here. You learned to network and make contacts with people you needed to meet to advance your goals. You learned how to build a rapport with these people and to communicate your ideas and abilities in a convincing

141

manner. You learned to work simultaneously on three different job targets. You learned how to overcome rejection and frustration and to press on until you achieved your goal.

What you have learned is a new set of transferable skills that may be valuable to you as you pursue your new career. If you need to reach someone to propose a new project or venture, if part of your role involves generating new business or clients, or if you simply want to meet someone you believe will be a valuable contact, you know how to do it! These skills are yours forever. Don't forget to take advantage of them.

## *Never Worry About Having to Change Careers Again*

There is another significant benefit you gained by jumping ship. You know that because you have done it once, you can do it again — and again if you feel like it! In an uncertain economy, this should provide a measure of security and confidence.

Three years from now, things may sour in a way you could *never* have anticipated. Your company may be taken over by a competitor. Your industry may fall on bad times. The wonderful boss or colleague who enticed you to join your organization may have left, and been replaced by Ivan the Terrible. Or perhaps you reach the top of the learning curve and find yourself bored. You need to keep your skills fresh. You need to maximize your earning power during your prime earning years. And if you find yourself at a roadblock on any of these counts, it may well be time to move on once again.

Many people have never learned how to engineer their own career transitions. They don't know where to begin, and will line up with everyone else at the headhunter's office, or poring over the ads in the careers section of the paper or on the Internet. If none of these efforts yield opportunities, they may simply decide to develop a coping strategy. They will continue to put up with things as they are, even though they're acutely aware that their current careers are no longer meeting their needs.

But for *you*, things are different. You have already been through a successful career transition once. You know it takes considerable time and effort to go through this again. You know exactly what is involved, and you know that it is not an entirely pleasant process. These are important things to know, because armed with this knowledge you can realistically assess how bad your current situation is relative to what would be required to make a transition. If, at the end of the day, you decide that it is time to make another transition, you know exactly how to go about it. Most important, you can go about it with confidence and experience. This knowledge truly allows you to be a "career entrepreneur." It gives you the freedom to escape a dead-end or unsatisfying job. Because you know the way out.

## *Payback Time*

There is something else that you will probably realize as you think back over the process. What you will realize is that many people helped you along the way.

Your friends put you in touch with their contacts, and those contacts — many of whom probably did not even know you — put you on to other contacts. Friends or references reviewed your draft résumés and critiqued your pitch. Experts you found through library research gave you valuable insights and even more contacts. People you had never met before agreed to have coffee with you. They listened to your pitch and gave you the benefit of their advice. In some cases, they put you on to other contacts who might have proved very useful. In other cases, they might have put the wheels in motion at their own organizations.

What you have learned about making a successful career transition is that nobody does it alone. The generosity that people have shown you in time, interest, ideas, and contacts is often quite overwhelming. It will undoubtedly be your most pleasant memory of the entire process. It often restores your faith in human nature at a time when you most need it!

So now that you have successfully jumped ship and are sailing off in an exciting new direction, it's payback time. Payback time begins by thanking the people who helped you along the way. Nothing elaborate is required. Just a warm call and a sincere thank you are usually more than enough for most people. They will be delighted to know that they helped you in some way to realize your goals!

But that is only the beginning, because payback time continues. It continues with others. You will undoubtedly find that making a successful career transition will become a source of interest and inspiration to other people who find themselves in career ruts. They will approach you asking your advice and whether you are happy that you made the change.

In the same way that so many people helped you, I urge you to use your experience in making a successful career transition to assist others. Share your process with them so that they know how to begin. Give them some insights into what you did that was particularly effective and what you would have done differently. Tell them how you coped with the frustrations inherent in a career transition.

If they have already developed job targets, provide them with the names and numbers of contacts that you may have in their chosen fields. If you feel comfortable, go a step further and offer to call these contacts on their behalf. Be available to kick around ideas during the course of their job search. You know only too well that this can be a lonely process at times and a word of encouragement (or a swift kick) is often badly needed. Be a coach; join a cheering section. You know only too well how much it will be appreciated.

In time, you may receive a call from someone explaining that they met you briefly at a conference or that they are a friend of someone you golf with. They will tell you they are considering a change of careers into your field and are doing some homework before they make their decision. They would like to meet with you — maybe over coffee — just to gain some insights that may help them with their decision. Would you be willing to have coffee with them?

You smile. You know the game. You know that this is a person who is trying to make a career transition. This person is interested in your organization and believes they have something to contribute. What they are really asking for is thirty minutes of your time to make their pitch.

You don't need any new employees. In fact, business has not been great this year. You can't see hiring this person even if they have just been awarded the Nobel prize in your field. A small voice urges, "Why waste your time and this person's time? Why build up his or her hopes when you know there is nothing here?"

And then another voice says, "If everyone took that approach, you would still be back at your rotten old job!" For all you know, this person may have an angle that could be of value to your organization even though you can't fathom it at the moment. Isn't it worth fifteen minutes of your time to at least check it out? And even if there is nothing at your organization, you can certainly offer some contacts if you think this person has potential. You have plenty of those yourself now! You can also offer your comments on their background and how suited they appear to be to the field. You can even take a quick look at their résumé and offer suggestions on how to improve it to highlight experience and skills that would be relevant to the transition.

You have a lot to offer. Check to ensure that the person has done their homework, that they are seriously interested in your field, and that they appear to be well-considered and professional. If you are convinced of those things — the very things that *you* did when approaching your prospects — and this person has asked if you will join them for coffee, the answer is always "Yes!" In fact, the only time that the answer is "No" is when you invite them to lunch instead.

# *Appendix: Checklist for Jumping Ship*

Networking Notebook Purchased    [  ]

## *Developing Job Targets*

Amount of $$$ you want to make:

$_____

Your passions/interests:

  1)_____
  2)_____
  3)_____
  4)_____
  5)_____

Your transferable skills/experience:

  1)_____
  2)_____
  3)_____

4)_____

5)_____

*Job Target*
A:_____

*Job Target*
B:_____

*Job Target*
C:_____

## Researching Job Targets

*Job Target A*
Directories:

1)_____

2)_____

3)_____

Magazines/Journals:

1)_____

2)_____

3)_____

Friends/associates who may have contacts in this field:

1)_____

Phone:_____

2)_____

Phone:_____

3)_____

Phone:_____

## *Job Target B*

Directories:

1)_____
2)_____
3)_____

Magazines/Journals:

1)_____
2)_____
3)_____

Friends/associates who may have contacts in this field:

1)_____
Phone:_____
2)_____
Phone:_____
3)_____
Phone:_____

## *Job Target C*

Directories:

1)_____
2)_____
3)_____

Magazines/Journals:

1)_____
2)_____
3)_____

Friends/associates who may have contacts in this field:

1)_____

Phone:_____

2)_____

Phone:_____

3)_____

Phone:_____

## *Your References*

1)_____

Phone:_____Called [ ]

2)_____

Phone:_____Called [ ]

3)_____

Phone:_____Called [ ]

4)_____

Phone:_____Called [ ]

5)_____

Phone:_____Called [ ]

6)_____

Phone:_____Called [ ]

7)_____

Phone:_____Called [ ]

8)_____

Phone:_____Called [ ]

9)_____

Phone:_____Called [ ]

10)_____

Phone:_____Called [ ]

## *Résumé Preparation*

Résumé prepared for Job Target A    [ ]
Résumé prepared for Job Target B    [ ]
Résumé prepared for Job Target C    [ ]

## *Identification of Target Organizations/ Companies to Approach*

ORGANIZATION/COMPANY          CONTACTS WHO CAN HELP YOU MEET PEOPLE THERE

### *Job Target A*

1)_____
2)_____
3)_____
4)_____
5)_____

### *Job Target B*

1)_____
2)_____
3)_____
4)_____
5)_____

### *Job Target C*

1)_____
2)_____
3)_____
4)_____
5)_____

## Event Networking Opportunities

List here any seminars, speeches, courses, or other events that might help you to learn more about and/or make contacts in each of your Job Target fields.

EVENT                                    DATE

### Job Target A

1)_____

2)_____

3)_____

### Job Target B

1)_____

2)_____

3)_____

### Job Target C

1)_____

2)_____

3)_____

## Other Networking Contacts

Friends    [  ]

Classmates from university/college    [  ]

Former co-workers    [  ]

Members of professional associations you belong to  [  ]

Family members    [  ]

Classmates from night courses/professional
    development courses  [  ]

Professors/teachers from university/college [ ]

Professors/teachers from night courses/professional
  development courses [ ]

People from clubs/volunteer organizations you belong to [ ]

People you know through sports or other activities  [ ]

Neighbours  [ ]

Classmates from high school/other classes  [ ]

Spouse's friends/associates  [ ]

Service providers:

  Broker    [ ]

  Hairstylist  [ ]

  Dentist  [ ]

  Doctor  [ ]

  Cleaning Person  [ ]

  Lawyer  [ ]

  Personal Trainer  [ ]

  Others: _____ [ ]

  _____ [ ]

Experts identified from library research

1)_____ [ ]

2)_____ [ ]

3)_____ [ ]


### *Developing Your "Pitch"*

Pitch developed for Job Target A  [ ]
Pitch rehearsed for Job Target A  [ ]

Pitch developed for Job Target B  [ ]
Pitch rehearsed for Job Target B  [ ]

Pitch developed for Job Target C  [ ]
Pitch rehearsed for Job Target C  [ ]

## Coach/Cheering Section

Coach:_____

No Coach [  ]

Cheering Section

1)_____

2)_____

3)_____

## Target Date

Date on which you will start your new job/career:

_____

# *Index*